THE STUDENT HANDBOOK

FOR

GREAT BOOKS
1 and 2

Department of English
Auburn University
Second Edition, 1998-2000

SIMON & SCHUSTER CUSTOM PUBLISHING

Cover Photograph: Cater Hall, Auburn University
Courtesy of Auburn University Photographic Services

Excerpts taken from:

The Working Writer by Toby Fulwiler
Copyright © 1995 by Prentice-Hall, Inc.
Simon & Schuster Company / A Viacom Company
Upper Saddle River, New Jersey 07458

This special edition published in cooperation with
Simon & Schuster Custom Publishing.

Printed in the United States of America

10 9 8 7 6 5 4 3 2 1

Please visit our website at www.sscp.com

ISBN 0-536-01578-3

BA 98425

SIMON & SCHUSTER CUSTOM PUBLISHING
160 Gould Street/Needham Heights, MA 02494
Simon & Schuster Education Group

Table of Contents

Chapter 1
Introduction: About Great Books

Where did our core curriculum come from? Near the end of the 1980s, looking toward a new millennium and new challenges for Auburn graduates, the Auburn University Board of Trustees together with the university faculty and administration, set out to rethink its undergraduate curriculum. Working through the University Senate Core Curriculum Commission, they considered together what Auburn students would need in order to become well-educated men and women—the citizens, leaders, problem solvers, and creative minds of the future.

They would need specialized knowledge and skills, of course, acquired in their majors, through advanced curricula, and professional programs. But their university experience should also equip all students, the Commission reasoned, with some essential skills and a broad, shared understanding of the world in its diversity. To achieve this, students would need a knowledge of the past and an appreciation for the arts. They would need an understanding of ethical issues and of how ethical and political decisions are made. They would need some understanding of science and mathematics, both their theory and their application. They would need some understanding of how individuals and societies work. They would need opportunities to read and talk together about important works of literature, philosophy, and history. They would need to be able to reason well and communicate effectively.

With these goals in mind, the Commission developed a set of recommendations which were adopted in modified form by the Auburn University Board of Trustees. The new 61-hour core curriculum was implemented in 1991. About one-third of the core hours established by the Commission and the Trustees are in English courses—freshman composition (10 hours), Great Books 1 (5 hours) and Great Books 2 (5 hours). These four courses form a coherent sequence through the freshman and sophomore years so that students extend their knowledge and refine their skills as they grow academically and intellectually.

What *is* Great Books? The Great Books sequence isn't primarily about the history of ideas or the history of cultures, though these are important ways of understanding some of the texts we study. It isn't a survey—an attempt to cover a particular period of literary history or certain key texts—though by the time your finish you will have come to know some important works and something of the world they come out of. Instead, the courses emphasize the vital and closely related skills of reading and writing at an advanced level.

A sophomore course taught in sections of approximately thirty students, Great Books gives you an unprecedented opportunity to read widely, to consider closely, to engage in sustained conversation with your peers, and your teacher, to develop or enhance your ability to analyze texts, and to write persuasively about your ideas. These interpretive abilities not only enrich our

1

lives and deepen our thinking, they also form the basis for many real-world skills and professional activities.

What *are* the great books? Some of the texts you read in Great Books have been thought of for a long time as important and worthy of study. When you read a story like Homer's *Odyssey*, a philosophical work like Plato's *Republic*, or a novel like Jane Austen's *Pride and Prejudice*, you join many generations of readers who have thought about and taken pleasure in them. These works are often thought of as "foundational" in Western civilization; they have helped to shape the way we think and act, the way we understand both the past and the present.

But like all fields of study, the study of literature has been expanded and energized by new knowledge. Some of the texts you read in Great Books are ones people of an earlier generation will never have heard of; they are works whose greatness has yet to be tried out and discovered by the students who encounter them. Works such as Frederick Douglass's *Narrative*, Leslie Silko's "Yellow Woman," and Chinua Achebe's *Things Fall Apart* reflect the diversity of our world and bring us voices—of minority writers, of women, of non-Western cultures—which are new and exciting.

Working within established guidelines, individual teachers choose readings for their sections of Great Books. Some make their selections from an anthology such as the *Norton Anthology of World Masterpieces* while others prefer to work with individual texts. In either case, teachers try to select works which have a lot to offer students and which provide the kinds of challenges which can lead to rewarding experiences for readers and to stimulating class discussion.

While you are taking Great Books you will probably develop your own criteria and your own sense of what qualities make a work great.

Who teaches Great Books? Most Great Books teachers are professors, instructors, or advanced doctoral students in English; others may be faculty from the departments of Foreign Languages, History, or other related fields. The Great Books faculty is large and diverse; their varied interests and areas of expertise, together with their commitment to common objectives, help to keep the course a vital one.

Chapter 2
Course Policies and Procedures

Objectives

As the English core courses following Freshman Composition and pre-requisite to the junior-level writing course, the sophomore Great Books courses further develop the related skills of careful reading and effective writing. Additionally, by engaging students in analysis and discussion of important written texts, Great Books enables students to participate in an ongoing dialogue about many of the intellectual and emotional issues which are central to being human.

Readings in Great Books 1 and 2

Each Great Books instructor chooses the works his or her classes will read. Some teachers use individual texts while others use an anthology of world literature and still others supplement an anthology with one or more individual texts. You should consult the course syllabus for information on the texts for your section, noting especially any information about which edition or translation is required.

The European Renaissance provides a rough chronological division between the two courses. Great Books 1 draws texts from ancient, medieval, and Renaissance cultures. Great Books 2 looks at works from the Enlightenment, the nineteenth century, and the twentieth century. Great Books teachers are also encouraged to represent cultural diversity, including at least one work in English and one not originally in English, at least one work by a woman, and at least one work by a member of a minority group within Western culture or a work by a member of a non-Western culture.

Writing Assignments

You should expect to write a minimum of 2400 words to be graded and returned before the last day of class. Because writing is an important mode of learning in Great Books, you should also expect to do a substantial amount of informal writing as part of your daily work for the course. Your writing assignments may include creative, analytical, or interpretive projects; in any case they will ask you to do more than merely summarize a work you are reading. Each class should require either [1] two longer papers or [2] one longer paper and a full revision which will be treated as a separate assignment.

Your teacher will provide you with written instructions or topics for these papers. Be sure your essays observe these guidelines and follow the assignment your instructor has given. Papers which fail to carry out the assignment may be given a grade of zero.

All of your written work for Great Books should show careful attention not only to ideas but to grammar, syntax, and style. It should be carefully proofread. Unless your instructor indicates otherwise, it should be typed. For information on resources which may help you with your papers, see "Resources for Great Books Students."

Exams

Great Books courses include supervised midterm and final examinations. These will include a substantial writing component.

Grades

Your Great Books teacher will indicate on the syllabus how your final grade for the course will be determined. For more information about the grades on your written work, see "What Essay Grades Mean."

Attendance

You should attend all classes. After a student's fifth unexcused absence, the instructor may assign a course grade of "FA" (failure because of absences). If you don't bring your text to class you can't participate in an informed way in the discussion and you may be counted absent for that class meeting.

Absences may be excused for reasons listed in the "Class Attendance Policy" in the *Tiger Cub*. These include:

a. Illness of the student or serious illness of a member of the student's family.
b. The death of a member of the student's immediate family.
c. Trips for members of the student organizations sponsored by an academic unit, trips for University classes, and trips for participation in intercollegiate athletic events. When feasible, the student must notify the instructor prior to the occurrence of such absences.
d. Religious holidays. Students are responsible for notifying the instructor in writing of anticipated absences due to their observance of such holidays.
e. Subpoena for court appearance.
f. Any other reason the instructor deems appropriate.

Excuses should be presented on the first day you return to class after an absence. Your teacher may request appropriate verification for an excuse.

You are responsible for initiating arrangements to make up work due to excused absences.

Assigned Work

You are expected to carry out all assigned work in the course. The due date for any written work is part of the assignment itself; your teacher may specify a penalty for late work.

Reading Quizzes and Other Daily Work

Quizzes and other daily assignments are an important part of your work for the course and may make up a substantial percentage of your grade for the quarter. Your teacher will indicate on the syllabus how quizzes and daily work will factor in to your overall grade. If you are absent and do not have an excuse, you may receive a grade of zero for the day's quiz or other daily assignment. If you are late, you may miss part or all of that day's quiz and lose points as a result.

Academic Honesty

The Student Academic Honesty Code is printed each year in the *Tiger Cub*. Great Books students should familiarize themselves with the code and refer to it, or to their instructor, with any questions they may have about academic honesty.

Of particular importance for Great Books students is the following section (D) of the code, which prohibits:

The submission of themes, essays, term papers, tests, design projects, similar requirements or parts therof that are not the work of the student submitting them. When direct quotations are used, they should be indicated, and when the ideas of another are incorporated into a paper, they must be appropriately acknowledged. Almost every student has heard the term "plagiarism." Nevertheless, there is a danger of failing to recognize either its full meaning or its seriousness. In starkest terms, plagiarism is stealing—using the words or ideas of another, as if they were one's own. If, for example, another person's complete sentence, syntax, key words, or the specific or unique ideas and information are used, one must give that person credit through proper documentation or recognition, as through the use of footnotes.

You are responsible for asking your teacher any questions you may have about honest use of sources or proper documentation. Guidelines for ethical and appropriate use of sources for research papers appear later in this book in the chapter "Documenting Sources."

Prerequisites. To be eligible for Great Books 1, you must be a sophomore and have completed the freshman composition requirement, earned advanced placement credit, or have received transfer credit for the freshman composition course at another school. To be eligible for Great Books 2, you must have sophomore standing, freshman composition credit, and Great Books 1 or its equivalent in transfer from another school. *If you are not eligible for the course but take it anyway, you may be removed from the roll after the fact by the Provost's Office of the Registrar; if this happens you will receive no credit for the course.* Only deans or department heads can waive eligibility requirements. If you are uncertain about your eligibility for Great Books, check with your academic advisor.

Students with Disabilities. All Auburn students are entitled to full access to courses, course materials, services, and activities offered by the university. If you have a disability and require accommodations in a Great Books course, you should make an appointment at the beginning of the quarter to discuss these with the instructor. For more information about disabilities services and accommodations, contact Dr. Kelly Haynes, Director, Program for Students with Disabilities, 844-2096.

Chapter 3
What Essay Grades Mean

A: This is an excellent paper, an innovative, creative, and perceptive response to the assignment. The purpose is specific, and the clearly focused thesis is marked by some depth or breadth of insight. The support is not only interesting and relevant but boldly thought-provoking. The careful organization is not only markedly clear and coherent, but also reflects a particularly apt response to the rhetorical situation. The style demonstrates the high competence of the B paper as well as exhibiting finesse through the writer's skillful use of stylistic elements to achieve specific goals.

B: This paper goes beyond a routine response to the assignment. The thesis reflects some originality or excites the curiosity of the audience. The development includes substantive support that is interesting, relevant, and complete. The organization is clear, coherent, and well suited to purpose and audience. Sentence structure shows variety, word choice is well suited to audience and purpose, and transitions function effectively to give the paper unity. The essay is generally free of distracting errors in grammar and mechanics.

C: This paper carries out the assignment in a competent way. While the C paper advances a reasonable thesis and offers some relevant support, these may be expressed in vague generalities or predictable and conventional ways. The pattern of organization is recognizable to the reader but may be formulaic or may not be the best for the purpose or audience of the paper. The voice and tone are generally appropriate. The style is essentially readable: there are few really awkward sentences; few serious errors in wording; and few, if any, glaring errors in grammar and mechanics. The C paper typically lacks variety of sentence structure, transitions are often inadequate, and word choice may be imprecise or cliched.

D: This is a paper that begins to meet the requirements of the assignment but is flawed in one or more of the following ways. The purpose may be confused or too general. The thesis may not be limited enough or clear enough. The support offered may not be wholly accurate or relevant, but in any case is far from sufficient. The organization may be unclear or confusing. The voice and tone may be inconsistent or somewhat inappropriate. And the style makes it difficult for the reader to understand what is being said: the sentence structure is at times awkward; the word choice is vague or ambiguous; and the number of grammatical or mechanical mistakes is sufficient to be distracting to the reader.

F: The failing paper does not meet the requirements of the assignment or has several interrelated flaws in purpose, support, organization, voice and tone, and style; and it is the combination of these distracting flaws that renders the paper essentially ineffective. Among the most serious flaws are lack of a purpose and/or lack of a controlling thesis that is clear, suitably limited, and on the assigned topic; almost total lack of support; absence of any apparent organizational or developmental plan; a voice or tone that alienates the audience; and a style that is unreadable either because of vagueness and imprecision or because of the number and magnitude of deviations from the conventions of edited American English.

Chapter 4
Resources for Great Books Students

The English Center, 3183 Haley Center, is staffed by faculty and graduate students and offers several kinds of assistance. Tutors in the English Center will:

1. Coach you on techniques to improve your writing process and help you become more confident and competent writers.
2. Help you learn basic grammar and mechanics.
3. Explain the principles of composition when you need help in addition to what your instructor provides.
4. Discuss your ideas about an essay assignment and help you arrive at a proper organizational plan for the essay. You should bring your assignment sheet with you to the English Center if you are seeking this kind of help.
5. Read your completed paper and tell you if it contains grammatical or mechanical errors, but without specifying where those errors are in the paper. It is your responsibility to proofread and edit your own papers but English Center tutors will help you learn to do this effectively.

There are some things English Center tutors won't do. These include editing, pointing out specific errors, rewriting sentences, or making corrections in your papers. They are also asked not to interpret texts or passages for you. English Center staff will not discuss the grade your instructor has assigned or predict what grade a paper will receive.

The English Center Hours will be posted each quarter.

Ralph Brown Draughon Library, Humanities Department, is a source of information on virtually every topic addressed in Great Books. Through reference books, regular books, periodicals, and on-line databases, the library gives you ways to learn more about the texts you are reading or about the times and places in which those texts were written. You may use these to gain background information (Who *are* all these Greek gods Homer mentions in his *Odyssey?* What do we know about Jane Austen's life?), to learn what others have had to say about a work you are studying, or to pursue new avenues of inquiry.

Some students find it interesting and useful to spend some time exploring the library on their own. The **Humanities Staff** can help you refine a general interest or question into an effective search for information. They can often point you to good sources or suggest places you might go for some focused browsing. Particularly during daytime hours you can get prompt, excellent help by going to the Humanities Reference Desk.

Your teacher may also be able to suggest library sources and help you develop a research plan or formulate a question for research.

The Internet is a rapidly-expanding, ever-changing source of information and help for Great Books students. Using search engines such as Yahoo, Veronica, Web Crawler, and others, students with Internet capabilities can gain access to a wide variety of materials, texts, reference tools, and databases.

Some of these will provide you with useful background information or help in reading; they may also help you develop and research a paper or project. A Norse Mythology home page, for instance, might supplement the footnotes in your text and allow you to learn more about the figures and the stories associated with the Norse saga your class is reading. You might locate an alternative translation of the *Odyssey*, a map of Ancient Greece, or photographs of ancient ruins to help you envision Homer's world. You might set out to learn more about the colonization of Africa or child labor laws in England or early twentieth-century painting in order to more fully understand a work you are reading in Great Books 2. While most of these materials are also available in the library, the Internet offers ready access from dorms, apartments, and computer labs and may help you discover some new paths for exploration.

When you use Internet materials in your written work, you take on the same ethical responsibilities as you would with any other source. That is, if you use someone else's words, ideas, information, or organization, you must indicate that clearly to your reader by citing the source. It doesn't matter whether these materials come from databases, home pages, bulletin boards, electronic lecture halls, or other sites, they must be documented. The forms for documenting electronic sources are still developing; your teacher can give you guidelines about how to do this as well as about where to look for useful information. More importantly, you should consult your teacher with any questions you may have about the ethics of using Internet resources.

A second caution for Internet users. Most scholarly books and journal articles go through a careful process of review and evaluation by other scholars in the field before they are published; readers can thus be fairly confident that the materials and ideas they find in such books and articles are sound and are based on acceptable methods and accurate information. On the Internet there is not yet a widely observed process of editorial review or evaluation. Anyone is free to publish ideas or information on the Internet, regardless of quality or accuracy. This means that when you use Internet resources, you will need to use good judgment, checking them against more traditional refereed sources and using your own knowledge to evaluate their quality.

Finally, you may want to use the Internet to converse with your teacher or your classmates. E-mail offers an informal, readily accessible way for you to communicate your questions and ideas and even to participate in electronic discussions. Your Great Books teacher may give you his or her e-mail address and encourage you to use this form of communication.

Other Resources: The **Tiger Cub** provides information on university services such as advising, computer labs, recreational facilities, and student organizations; it also provides a comprehensive description of student rights and responsibilities. The **Auburn Bulletin** contains information on university, college, and department requirements and on academic regulations concerning transfer credit, exams, special programs of study, and other matters. You should have current copies of each of these books.

Your Instructor: Your most important resource for Great Books is your teacher. All Great Books faculty keep regular office hours and will schedule appointments at other times as needed. Many hold conferences at mid-quarter or before a paper is due. You can ask your teacher for help understanding a particular text or for guidance about how to improve your performance in the course. You can ask for assistance in finding information, developing your ideas for a paper, or confronting a new kind of assignment. Both in and out of the classroom your questions are an important part of the learning process.

Your teacher should also be the first person you consult if you have a concern about a grade or some other aspect of the course. Problems can often be resolved at this level. Those which cannot be settled between teacher and student should be brought to the Director of Great Books.

Chapter 5
College Reading

Now that I'm in college, I would like to be challenged when I read
and write, to think, and ask good questions, and find good answers.
— WOODY

TO READ AND WRITE WELL IN COLLEGE means to read and write critically. In fact, a major goal of most college curricula is to train students to be critical readers, writers, and thinkers so they can carry those habits of mind into the larger culture beyond college. What, you may ask, does it mean to be critical? How does being a critical reader, writer, and thinker differ from being a plain, ordinary, everyday reader, writer, and thinker?

Being critical in writing means making distinctions, developing interpretations, and drawing conclusions that stand up to thoughtful scrutiny by others. Being critical in reading means knowing how to analyze these distinctions, interpretations, and conclusions. Becoming a critical thinker, then, means learning to exercise reason and judgment whenever you encounter the language of others or generate language yourself.

Most of *The Working Writer* explores strategies for helping you become an accomplished critical writer. This chapter, however, explores strategies for helping you become a more accomplished critical reader and emphasizes as well the close relationship between critical reading and critical writing.

WRITING 1

Describe yourself as a reader, answering some of these questions along the way: How often do you read on your own? What kinds of reading do you do when the choice of reading material is up to you? Where and when do you most commonly do your reading? What is the last book you read on your own? Who is your favorite author? Why?

READING TO UNDERSTAND

Before you can read critically, you need to understand what you're reading. To understand a text, you need to know something about it already. It's virtually impossible to read and understand material that is entirely new. You need to understand enough of the text and its ideas to fit them into a place in your own mind where they make sense and connect with other information you already know. The following example will explain what I mean.

Reading Field Hockey

Have you ever watched a game for which you did not know the rules? Not long ago I saw a field hockey game for the first time, and for much of the game I was fairly confused. Players ran up and down a field swinging bent sticks at a little rubber ball. I guessed — because I knew something of other field games like soccer — that the objective was to drive the ball down the field with a stick and hit it into the opponent's net. But I didn't understand why the referee blew her whistle so often, or why the team lined up different way at different times, or what the offensive and defensive strategies were.

In other words, I saw the same game as many fans around me, but I understood less of it. I was unable to "read" it because I had do little prior knowledge. However, the more I watched, the more I began to learn. Even though field hockey was new to me, I began to make associations with what I knew about similar games, including ice hockey and soccer. Soon I found myself making predictions based on this associational knowledge, and many of these proved to be correct. I predicted, for instance, that when a player hit the ball in the air instead of along the ground, a whistle would blow, for this was a foul. I learned later that this foul was called "high sticking." The more games I saw, the more I predicted, learned, and understood — about "high sticking," "strikers," "corners," "long and short hits," and the like.

By midseason, I found myself correctly anticipating the referee's calls, second-guessing various offensive and defensive strategies, and understanding the scores. When I was puzzled by something, I also learned who among the other fans to ask for help. I learned to read this strange text, field hockey, by watching the game closely, by comparing it to what I already knew, by asking questions, by making trial-and-error guesses, and by consulting expert sources.

By season's end, I cheered good plays and shook my head at bad ones. I applauded certain coaching strategies but questioned (quietly) other ones. In fact, I began to feel knowledgeable enough about the game to answer other people's questions about what was happening, which reinforced my own sense of expertise and gave me confidence that I had become an expert of a sort. In the end, I actually learned enough not only to comprehend what I saw but to analyze, interpret, and evaluate it as well. I moved, in other words, from a mere watcher to a critical observer of field hockey.

Understanding Field Hockey

Let's look again at the strategies I employed to understand the game of field hockey.

First, I watched the game closely and *identified* what I saw. I looked at the number of players; their uniforms and equipment; the size, shape, and markings on the field; the action as the players ran up and down the field hitting the little rubber ball with their bent sticks; and the pauses, interruptions, cheers, and whistles. I noticed that the field resembled, in size, shape, and surface, a football or soccer field and that at each end was a net-like cage defended by a well-padded player who looked a bit like a goalie in ice hockey.

Second, I *questioned* what I saw. Why did the players line up in certain ways? What infractions caused the whistle to blow? How did they keep score? How long did a game last? Some of these I answered through further observation, and some were answered by other fans.

Third, I *predicted* (hypothesized) about what would happen in the game if my assumptions were correct. I guessed, for instance, that field hockey operated something like ice hockey. I then predicted that whenever the little rubber ball was driven into the opponent's net a score would be recorded.

Fourth, I *tested* my predictions and found that, yes, a score was recorded whenever the ball was driven into the opposing team's net — with some exceptions.

Finally, I *confirmed* my hunches by consulting expert sources and to find out more about the game. For instance, one time when I saw a ball driven into a opponent's net, a score was *not* recorded; I asked why and was told that a penalty had nullified the score. That made sense since the same thing occurs in football, soccer, and ice hockey, but I had not yet learned to recognize what constitutes a penalty in field hockey.

In other words, the more I observed and studied, the more I understood. The more I understood, the more I could assess what I saw, discuss it, and make critical judgments about it.

Reading Written Texts

The same strategies that taught me to "read" field hockey games apply to reading written texts. To understand a text, you need some context for the new ideas you encounter, some knowledge of the text's terms and ideas and of the rules that govern the kind of writing you're reading.

It would be difficult to read Mark Twain's novel *The Adventures of Huckleberry Finn* with no knowledge of American geography, the Mississippi River, or the institution of slavery. It would also be difficult to read a biology textbook chapter about photosynthesis but know nothing of plants, cell structure, or chemical reactions. The more you know, the more you learn; the more you learn, the more careful and critical your reading, writing, and thinking will be.

Many college instructors will ask you to read about subjects that are new to you; you won't be able to spend much time reading about what you already know. To graduate, you've got to keep studying new subjects that require, first, that you understand what you read and, second, that you can critically assess and write about this new understanding. As you move through the college curriculum, you will find yourself an expert reader in some disciplines, a novice reader in others, and neither expert nor novice in the rest — often during the same semester.

If getting a college degree requires that you read one unfamiliar text after another, how can you ever learn to read successfully? How do you create a context, learn a background, and find the rules to help you read unfamiliar texts in unfamiliar subject areas? What strategies or shortcuts can speed up the learning process? Let's consider some strategies for doing this.

Understanding Written Texts

As an experiment, read the following short opening paragraph from an eight-paragraph *New York Times* story entitled "Nagasaki, August 9, 1945." When you have finished, pause for a few moments, and think about (1) what you learned from it, (2) how you learned what you learned, and (3) what the rest of the story will be about.

> In August 1945, I was a freshman at Nagasaki Medical College. The ninth of August was a clear, hot, beautiful summer day. I left my lodging house, which was one and one half miles from the hypocenter, at eight in the morning, as usual, to catch a tram car. When I got to the tram stop, I found that it had been derailed in an accident. I decided to return home. I was lucky. I never made it to school that day.
>
> — MICHAITO ICHIMARU

How did you do? It is possible that your reasoning went something like mine, which I reconstructed here. Note, however, that although the following sequence presents ideas one after the other, that's not how it seemed to happen when I read the passage for the first time. Instead, meaning seemed to occur in flashes, simultaneously and unmeasurably. Even as I read a sentence for the first time, I found myself reading backward as much as forward to check my understanding. Here are the experiences that seemed to be happening.

1. I read the first sentence carefully, noticing the year 1945 and the name of the medical college, "Nagasaki." My prior historical knowledge kicked in, as I *identified* Nagasaki, Japan, as the city on which the United States dropped an atomic bomb at the end of World War II — though I did not remember the precise date.
2. I noticed the city and the date, August 9, and wondered if that was when the bomb was dropped. I *asked* (silently), Is this a story about the bomb?

3. Still looking at the first sentence, a reference to the writer's younger self ("I was a freshman"), I guessed that the author was present at the dropping of this bomb. I *predicted* that this would be a survivor's account of the bombing of Nagasaki.

4. The word *hypocenter* in the third sentence made me pause again; the language seemed oddly out of place next to the "beautiful summer day" described in the second sentence. I *questioned* what the word meant. Though I didn't know exactly, it sounded like a technical term for the place where the bomb went off. Evidence was mounting that the narrator may have lived one and a half miles from the exact place where the atomic bomb detonated.

5. In the next to the last sentence of the paragraph, the author says that he was "lucky" to miss the tram. Why, unless something unfortunate happened to the tram, would he consider missing it "lucky"? I *predicted* that had the author gone to school "as usual" he would have been closer to the hypocenter, which I now surmise was at Nagasaki Medical College.

6. I then *tested* my several predictions by reading the rest of the story — which you, of course, could not do. My predictions proved correct: Michaito Ichimaru's story is a firsthand account of witnessing and surviving the dropping of the bomb, which in fact killed all who attended the medical college, a quarter of a mile from the hypocenter.

7. Finally, out of curiosity, I looked up Nagasaki in the *Columbia Desk Encyclopedia* and *confirmed* that 75,000 people were killed by this second dropping of an atomic bomb, on August 9, 1945; the first bomb had been exploded just three days earlier, on August 6, at Hiroshima.

You'll notice that in my seven-step example some parts of the pattern of identifying/questioning/predicting/testing/confirming occur more than once, perhaps simultaneously, and not in a predictable order. This is a slow-motion description — not a prescription or formula — of the activities that occur in split seconds in the minds of active, curious readers. No two readers would — or could — read this passage in exactly the same way, because no two readers are ever situated identically in time and space, with identical training, knowledge, or experience to enable them to do so. However, my reading process may be similar enough to yours that the comparison will hold up: reading is a messy, trial-and-error process that depends as much on prior knowledge as on new information to lead to understanding.

Whether you read new stories or watch unfamiliar events, you commonly make meaning by following a procedure something like mine, trying to identify what you see, question what you don't understand, make and test predictions about meaning, and consult authorities for confirmation or information. Once you know how to read successfully for basic comprehension, you are ready to read critically.

> **WRITING 2**
>
> In a book you have been assigned to read for one of your courses, find a chapter that has not yet been covered in class. Read the first page of this chapter and then stop. Write out any predictions you have about where the rest of the chapter is going. (Ask yourself, for example, What is its main theme or argument? How will it conclude?) Finish reading the chapter and check its conclusion against your predictions. If your predictions were close, you are reading for understanding.

READING CRITICALLY

How people read depends on what they're reading; people read different materials in different ways. When they read popular stories and magazine articles for pleasure, they usually read not to be critical but to understand and enjoy. In fact, while pleasure readers commonly go through a process similar to the one described in the last section — identifying, questioning, predicting, and testing — they usually do so rapidly and unconsciously. Since such reading is seldom assigned in college courses, whether they go further to confirm and expand their knowledge depends solely on their time, energy, and interest.

When people read college textbooks, professional articles, technical reports, and serious literature, they read more slowly and carefully to assess the worth or validity of an author's ideas, information, argument, or evidence. The rest of this chapter describes the strategies that lead readers from *understanding* texts to *critically* interpreting and evaluating them, paying special attention to the strategies of *previewing, responding,* and *reviewing.*

Although critical reading is described here as a three-stage process, it should be clear that these activities seldom happen in a simple one-two-three order. For example, one of the best ways to preview a text is to respond to it briefly as you read it the first time; as you respond, you may find yourself previewing and reviewing, and so on. But if you're not engaging in all three activities at some time, you're not getting as much from your reading as you could.

Previewing Texts

To be a critical reader, you need to be more than a good predictor. In addition to following the thread of an argument, you need to evaluate its logic, weigh its evidence, and accept or reject its conclusion. You read actively, searching for information and ideas that you both understand and can make use of — to further your own thinking, speaking, or writing. To move from understanding to critical awareness, you plan to read a text more than once and more than one way — which is why critical readers *preview* texts before reading them from start to finish.

To understand a text critically, plan to preview before you read, and make previewing the first of several steps needed to fully appraise the value of the text.

First Questions

Ask questions of a text (a book, an article, a report) from the moment you pick it up. Ask first questions to find general, quickly gleaned information, such as that provided by skimming the title, subtitle, subheads, table of contents, or preface.

- What does the title suggest?
- What is the subject?
- What does the table of contents promise?
- What is emphasized in chapter titles or subheads?
- Who is the author? (Have I heard of him or her?)
- What makes the author an expert or authority?
- How current is the information in this text?
- How might this information help me?

You may not ask these first questions methodically, in this order, or write down all your answers, but if you're a critical reader you'll ask these types of questions before you commit too much time to reading the whole text. If your answers to these first questions suggest that the text is worth further study, you can continue with the preview process.

Second Questions

Once you've determined that a book or article warrants further critical attention, it's very helpful to read rapidly selected parts of it to see what they promise. Skim reading leads to still more questions, the answers to which you will want to capture on note cards or in a journal.

- Read the prefatory material: What can I learn from the book jacket, foreword, or preface?
- Read the introduction, abstract, or first page: What theme or thesis is promised?
- Read a sample chapter or subsection: Is the material about what I expect?
- Scan the index or chapter notes: What sources have informed this text? What names do I recognize?
- Note unfamiliar words or ideas: Do I have the background to understand this text?
- Consider: Will I have to consult other sources to obtain a critical understanding of this one?

In skim reading, you make predictions about coverage, scope, and treatment and about whether the information seems pertinent or useful for your purpose.

Previewing *Iron John*

One of my students has just given me a book called *Iron John*. To find out more about the book, I previewed it by asking first questions and second questions, the answers to which I've reproduced here for illustration.

ANSWERS TO FIRST QUESTIONS

- The title *Iron John* is intriguing and suggests something strong and unbreakable.
- I already know and admire the author, Robert Bly, for his insightful poetry, but I've never read his prose.
- The table of contents raises interesting questions, but doesn't tell me much about where the book is going:

1. The Pillow and the Key
2. When One Hair Turns Gold
3. The Road of Ashes, Descent, and Grief
4. The Hunger for the King in Time with No Father
5. The Meeting with the God-Woman in the Garden

ANSWERS TO SECOND QUESTIONS

- The jacket says, "*Iron John* is Robert Bly's long-awaited book on male initiation and the role of the mentor, the result of ten years' work with men to discover truths about masculinity that get beyond the stereotypes of our popular culture."
- There is no introduction or index, but the chapter notes in the back of the book (260–67) contain the names of people Bly used as sources in writing the book. I recognize novelist D. H. Lawrence, anthropologist Mircea Eliade, poet William Blake, historian/critic Joseph Campbell, and a whole bunch of psychologists — but many others I've never heard of. An intriguing mix.

This preview, which took maybe ten minutes, confirmed that *Iron John* is a book about men and male myths in modern American culture by a well-known poet writing a serious prose book in friendly style. Apparently, Bly not only will examine current male mythology but will make some recommendations about which myths are destructive, which constructive.

Previewing is only a first step in a process that now slows down and becomes more time-consuming and critical. As readers begin to seriously preview a text, they often make notes in the text's margin or in a journal or notebook to mark places for later review. In other words, before the preview stage of critical reading has ended, the *responding* stage has probably begun.

WRITING 3

Select any unfamiliar book about which you are curious and preview it, using the strategy of first and second questions discussed in this section. Stop after ten minutes, and write what you know about the text.

Responding to Texts

Once you understand, through a quick critical preview, what a text promises, you need to examine it more slowly, evaluating its assumptions, arguments, evidence, logic, and conclusion. The best way to do this is to *respond*, or "talk back," to the text in writing.

Talking back can take many forms, from making margin notes to composing extensive notebook entries. Respond to passages that cause you to pause for a moment to reflect, to question, and read again, or to say Ah! or Ah ha! At all points of high interest, take notes.

If the text is informational, try to capture the statements that pull together or summarize ideas or are repeated. If the text is argumentative (and many of the texts you'll be reading in college will be), examine the claims the text makes about the topic and each piece of supporting evidence. If the text is literary (a novel, play, or poem), pay extra attention to language features such as images, metaphors, and crisp dialogue. In any text, notice words the author puts in boldface or italics — they have been marked for special attention.

Note what's happening to you as you read. Ask about the effect of the text on you: How am I reacting? What am I thinking and feeling? What do I like? What do I distrust? Do I know why yet? But don't worry too much now about answering all your questions. (That's where reviewing comes in.)

The more you write about something, the more you will understand it. Using a reading journal is a good way to keep your responses together in one place that you can return to when writing an essay or research paper. Write each response on a fresh page and include the day's date, the title, and author. Write any and all reactions you have to the text including summaries, notes on key passages, speculations, questions, answers, ideas for further research, and connections to other books or events in your life. Note especially ideas with which you agreed or disagreed. Explore ideas that are personally appealing. Record memorable quotations (with page numbers) as well as the reasons they strike you as memorable.

The following brief passage from Bly's *Iron John* is an example of a text to respond to.

> The dark side of men is clear. Their mad exploitation of earth resources, devaluation and humiliation of women, and obsession with tribal warfare are undeniable. Genetic inheritance contributes to their obsessions, but also culture and environment. We have defective mythologies that ignore masculine depth of feeling, assign men a place in the sky instead of earth, teach

obedience to the wrong powers, work to keep men boys, and entangle both men and women in systems of industrial domination that exclude both matriarchy and patriarchy. . . .

I speak of the Wild Man in this book, and the distinction between the savage man and the Wild Man is crucial throughout. The savage soul does great damage to soul, earth, and humankind; we can say that though the savage man is wounded he prefers not to examine it. The Wild Man, who has examined his wound, resembles a Zen priest, a shaman, or a woodsman more than a savage.

When you want to critically read a text such as this, do so with pen or pencil in hand. Mark places to examine further, but be aware that mere marking (underlining, checking, highlighting) does not yet engage you in a conversation with the text. To converse with the text, you need to actively engage in one or more of the following activities: probing, annotating, cross-referencing, and outlining. The following sections illustrate full responses for each activity; in reality, however, a reader would use no more than one or two of these techniques to critically examine a single text.

Probing

You probe a text when you raise critical questions and see if you can answer them. *Probing* is, in essence, asking deeper questions than those asked in previewing. What you ask will depend, of course, on your reason for reading in the first place. Here, for example, are the questions I raised about the *Iron John* passage:

- Bly refers to the dark side of men; does he ever talk about the dark side of women? How would women's darkness differ from men's? What evidence for either does he provide?
- Bly suggests that part of men's dark behavior is genetic, part cultural; where does he get this information? Does he think it's a 50/50 split?
- What "defective mythologies" is Bly talking about? Does he mean things like religion and politics, or is her referring to nursery rhymes and folktales?
- Bly generalizes in his opening sentence, "The dark side of men is clear" — in most sentences actually. Will subsequent chapters support these statements or are we asked to accept them on faith?
- I like the dimension Bly makes between "Wild" and "savage" men. Did he coin the terms or are they used pervasively in mythology in the same way? I wonder how sharp the line really is between the two.

Those are five good questions to ask about the passage; however, any other reader could easily think of five or more. These questions are "critical" in the sense that they not only request further information from the book — which all readers need to request — but also challenge the text's terms, statements, and sources to see if they will stand up under sharp scrutiny.

The questions are written in my own language. Using your own words helps in at least three ways: it forces you to articulate precisely; it makes the question *your* question; and it helps you remember the question for future use.

Annotating and Cross-Referencing

Annotating, or talking back to the author in the margins of the text, is an excellent way to make that text your own, a necessary step in understanding it fully. Annotating is easier if you have your own copy of the text — otherwise you can make your annotations on Post-It notes or in a notebook with page numbers marked. As a critical reader, you can annotate the following:

- Points of agreement and disagreement
- Exceptions and counterexamples
- Extensions and further possibilities
- Implications and consequences
- Personal associations and memories
- Connections to other texts, ideas, and courses
- Recurring images and symbols

To move beyond annotating (commenting on single passages) to *cross-referencing* (finding relationships among your annotations), devise a coding system to note when one annotation is related to another and thus identify and locate different patterns in the text. Some students write comments in different colored ink — red for questions, green for nature images, blue for speculations, and so on. Other students use numbers — 1 for questions, 2 for images, and so on.

In *Iron John,* for example, the term "Wild Man" occurs on pages 6, 8–12, 14, and 26–27, in other chapters, and in the title of the book's epilogue. A critical reader would mark all of these. In addition, the related term "Hairy Man" occurs on pages 5, 6, and 11, and so on. In cross-referencing, I noted in the margins when the two terms occurred together.

Outlining

Another way of talking back to a text is *outlining.* This involves simply writing out a condensed version of the opening sentence or topic sentence of each paragraph, capturing its essence, as I did for the two paragraphs from *Iron John:*

1. The dark side of men
2. The Savage Man versus the Wild Man

Of course, two paragraphs are simply a start; outlining ten or more paragraphs provides a real clue to the author's organizational pattern. Once you have outlined an article or chapter, you will remember that text better, be able to find key passages more quickly, and see larger patterns more easily.

WRITING 4

Keep a reading journal for one article, chapter, or book that you are assigned to read this semester. Be sure to write something in the journal after every reading session. In addition, annotate and cross-reference the text as you go along to see what patterns you can discover. Finally, make a paragraph outline of the text. Write about the result of these response methods in your journal. Did they help? Which ones worked best?

To *review* you need both to reread and to "re-see" a text, reconsidering its meaning and the ideas you have about it. You need to be sure that you grasp the important points within the text, but you also need to move beyond that to a critical understanding of the text as a whole. In responding, you started a conversation with the text so you could put yourself into its framework and context; in reviewing, you should consider how the book can fit into your own framework and context. Review any text you have previewed and responded to as well as anything you've written in response — journal entries, freewriting, annotations, outlines. Keep responding, talking back to the text, even as you review, writing new journal entries to capture your latest insights.

Reviewing can take different forms depending on how you intend to use the text — whether or not you are using it to write a paper, for example. In general, when reviewing a text you have to understand what it means, to interpret its meaning, to evaluate its soundness or significance, and to determine how to use it in your own writing.

Reviewing to Understand

Reviewing to understand means identifying and explaining in your own words the text's main ideas. This task can be simplified if you have outlined the text while responding or have cross-referenced your annotations to highlight relationships among ideas. In reviewing to understand, you can reread portions of articles that you previewed, considering especially abstracts, if there are any; first and last paragraphs; and sections entitled "Summary," "Observations," or "Conclusions." In a book, you can reconsider the table of contents, the introductory and concluding chapters, and central chapters that you recognize as important to the author's argument or theme.

Reviewing to Interpret

Reviewing to interpret means moving beyond an appreciation of what the text *says* and building your own theory of what the text *means*. An interpretation is an assertion of what you as a reader think the text is about.

In reviewing to interpret, look over any of your journal entries that articulate overall reactions to the text's main ideas. What did you see in the text?

Do you still have the same interpretation? Also reread key passages in the text, making sure that your interpretation is reasonable and is based on the text and is not a product of your imagination.

If you plan to write a critical paper about a text, it's a good idea to confirm your interpretation by consulting what others have said about that text. The interpretations of other critics will help put your own view in perspective as well as raise questions that may not have occurred to you. Try to read more than one perspective on a text. It is better to consult such sources in this reviewing stage, after you have established some views of your own, so that you do not simply adopt the view of the first expert you read.

Reviewing to Evaluate

Reviewing to evaluate means deciding whether you think the text accomplishes its own goals. In other words, is the text any good? Different types of texts should be judged on different grounds.

ARGUMENTS. Many texts you read in college make arguments about ideas, advancing certain *claims* and supporting those claims with *evidence*. A claim is a statement that something is true or should be done. Every claim in an argument should be supported by reliable and sufficient evidence.

At the responding stage, you probably started to identify and comment on the text's claims and evidence. In reviewing, you can ask the following questions to examine and evaluate each part of the argument to see whether it is sound:

- Is the claim based on facts? A *fact* is something that can be verified and that most readers will accept without question. (Fact: The title of the book is *Iron John*; the author is Robert Bly; it was published in 1990; the myth of Iron John is found in several ancient folktales that have been written down and can be found in libraries and so on.)
- Is the claim based on a credible inference? An *inference* is a conclusion drawn from an accumulation of facts. (Bly's inferences in *Iron John* about the warrior in modern man are based on his extensive study of ancient mythology. His inferences have a basis in the facts, but other readers might draw other inferences.)
- Is the claim based on opinion? An *opinion* reflects an author's personal beliefs and may be based on faith, emotion, or myth. Claims based on opinion are considered weak in academic writing. (Bly's "dark side of men" is metaphorical and not factual. Some readers would consider it a fair inference based on the savage history of humankind; others would dismiss it as Bly's opinion, based on emotion rather than on facts and careful reasoning.)

All three types of evidence — facts, inference, and opinions — have their place in argumentative writing, but the strongest arguments are those that are based on accurate facts and reasonably drawn inferences. Look out for opinions that are masquerading as facts and for inferences that are based on insufficient facts.

INFORMATIONAL TEXTS. In reviewing informational texts, like reviewing argumentative texts, you need to make sure that the facts are true, that inferences rely on facts, and that opinions presented as evidence are based on expertise, not emotion. Informational texts don't make arguments, but they do draw conclusions from the facts they present. You must decide whether there are enough reliable facts to justify these conclusions. Consider also whether you think the author is reliable and reasonable: Is the tone objective? Has all the relevant information been presented? Is this person an expert?

LITERATURE. Literary texts (short stories, poems, and plays) don't generally make arguments, but they do strive to be believable, to be enjoyable, and to be effective in conveying their themes. One way to evaluate literature is to reread journal entries in which you responded to the author's images, themes, or overall approach. Then look through the text again — guided by any annotations you've made — and ask whether you think the author's choices were good ones. Look in particular for repeated terms, ideas, or images that will help you see the pattern of the text as a whole. Evaluating literature is often very personal, relying on individual associations and responses, but the strongest critical evaluations are based on textual evidence.

Reviewing to Write

Reviewing a text to use in writing your own paper means locating specific passages to quote, paraphrase, or summarize in support of your own assertions about the text. When you quote, you use the exact language of the text; when you paraphrase, you restate the text in your own words; when you summarize, you reduce the text to a brief statement in your own words. When you identify a note card that contains a passage to quote, paraphrase, or summarize, make sure that you have recorded the page on which the passage occurs in the text so you can find it again and so you can prepare correct documentation. (See Chapter 19 for advice about using textual sources in your papers.)

READING AND WRITING

Reading and writing, like production and consumption, are two sides of the same coin. When you study one, you inevitably learn more about the other at the same time. The more you attend to the language of published writers, the more you will learn about your own language. The more you attend to your own written language, the more you will learn about the texts you read.

In fact, many of the reading strategies you use to understand and evaluate published texts work equally well when reading your own writing. You can preview, respond to, and review your own or your classmates' writing to gain a critical understanding of your writing and to discover strategies for effective revision.

SUGGESTIONS FOR WRITING AND RESEARCH

Individual

Select a short text. First read it quickly for understanding. Second, read it critically as described in this chapter. Finally, write a short (two-page) critical review of the text, recommending or not recommending it to other readers. (For more detailed information about writing critically about texts, see Chapter 14.)

Collaborative

As a class or in small groups, agree on a short text to read and write about according to the preceding directions. Share your reviews in small groups, paying particular attention to the claims and evidence each writer uses in his or her review. Rewrite the reviews based on the responses in the groups. (For more information about responding to others' texts, see Chapter 9.)

Chapter 6
Interpreting Texts

When I read, I've learned to ask a lot of questions, such as Who's telling the story? What's the character like? Why does a certain action happen? What do symbols mean? Things like that. But I never find as much meaning in the stories as my teachers do.

— *Diane*

WHEN YOU INTERPRET SOMETHING, you address the question What does it mean? When most of us encounter something new and interesting, we try to make sense of it by figuring out how it works, by comparing it to similar things, by analyzing our reactions to it, and by trying to determine why it affects us the way it does. Interpreting things is how we learn to understand and value them.

We usually think of texts as the written material found in books and periodicals. However, virtually all symbolic works can be considered texts open to interpretation — video and audio recordings, films, music and dance performances, exhibits, paintings, photographs, sculptures, advertisements, artifacts, and even whole cultures.

You are probably familiar with the reviews that are commonly written about these texts, such as a review in a newspaper or magazine telling you whether a film is worth seeing. A review is a form of interpretation that not only answers the interpretive question What does it mean? but also asks the evaluative question Is it good? Most interpretive essays in writing classes focus on written texts and are more interpretive than evaluative.

WRITING TO INTERPRET

Our initial reactions to a new text of any kind are often a jumble of impressionistic thoughts, feelings, and memories — seldom fully realized interpretations. To write an interpretive essay, you must take the time to analyze this jumble and develop a reasonable, systematic understanding of what the text means and why. Since all texts have more than one possible meaning and are open to more than one interpretation, in an interpretive essay you also try to make the best possible case that your reading is a good one and deserves attention.

A fully developed interpretation *explains* what the text says, in and of itself. It also *argues* for a particular interpretation of the text's meaning — what the text implies or suggests in a larger sense. Like any argument, an interpretive essay should be as persuasive as possible, but it can never be an absolute proof.

Interpretive essays, which are also called critical, analytical, or review essays, are among the most frequent college writing assignments. A typical assignment may ask you to interpret a poem, a story, an essay, a newspaper or magazine article, or even a historical document. Writing a good textual interpretation will require various writing strategies. To explain a text, you will usually have to describe its people and situations, summarize its events, and define important concepts or terms. You may also need to analyze the various parts of the text and explain how they work together as a whole, perhaps by comparing the text to others. To argue for your interpretation, you will have to develop a strong thesis and defend it with sound reasoning and effective evidence. In many cases, you will also be expected to evaluate the text's worth and reflect on its significance to you.

The following essay and the two responses to it, demonstrate the art of interpretive writing. It was written by Angel Fuster, a senior majoring in English and enrolled in an advanced writing class. After you have read his essay, study the various strategies for writing about it, as well as two essays — one objective and one subjective — written by first-year students who read and interpreted Angel's story.

While Fuster's essay is autobiographical and therefore nonfiction, many of the texts you will be asked to analyze in college will be fiction or poetry. But the techniques for interpreting works of fiction and nonfiction are the same.

Angelique's Letter
Angel Fuster

– 1 –

The letter is written on standard grade-school paper, the blue lines far enough apart for any kid to learn on. Her name, "Angelique," at the top of the page, is done in her fanciest style. But the characters are boxy and it looks as though they were done especially slow.

– 2 –

"Just like a nice restaurant's name," my nine-year-old sister said.
I wanted to say how proud I was that she was learning script, but instead replied, "Yeah, like those restaurants only rich white people go to."
She gazed at her name and smiled wishfully. "Yeah, if I was white, I'd make a restaurant with those letters."

"Don't worry, Mamma, if you go to college like me, you could get whatever you want."

I felt guilty for using her artistically written "Angelique" to teach her about racism, especially since I knew what I had said was a bit oversimplified and inaccurate. But what could I do? How could I ensure that she grows up questioning things? I had to keep her from getting pregnant and dropping out of school as many of her classmates will, as my older sister did, and as my mother before her. And she was already talking about boys.

– 3 –

The boys loved to talk about Sorada Rodriguez, but none loved her like I did. One day I walked up to her on the playground and, without thinking, took out my pencil and poked her in the thigh.

She was sent to the nurse. I waited after school and told her I was sorry, and she just gave me the worst stare and screamed at me.

I walked her the two blocks to her side of the projects without saying a word. When we got to the empty apartment, I kissed her on the mouth. Then, still without saying a word, she took off her clothes, like in the movies, and I took off mine. I was embarrassed because I had no hair and she had a lot.

– 4 –

I would have to get Angelique interested in important issues, things that would excite her, make her want to develop her mind so she would grow into a thinking person. My strategy was twofold: I would give her enormous pride in her people, then I would teach her to act on that pride to improve herself. But in order to keep her interested in these issues, I would have to show that they directly affect her, using every opportunity I could to bring up the subject.

– 5 –

"Chino, play Barbie with me. You could be her," Angelique said, holding up a blond doll dressed in a bikini bathing suit.

"No, I don't want her. I want the one with the black hair. It isn't fair that all the Barbies are blond. Black hair is beautiful too. They don't even make Puerto Rican Barbies."

She studied the long wiry blondness. "I wish they make Puerto Rican Barbies."

I felt like telling her I was only kidding.

– 6 –

Under "Angelique," her words are written in large print that allows only four or five words to fit between the pink margins.

Dear Chino,
  How are you doing?
  remember you said to write
  you a song or a story? Well, I
  am goging to write bouth of them.
  Are you happy?

32

Indeed, I was very happy. My plan to educate Angelique was working. Getting her to write was one step in encouraging her to be a thinking person. I knew that in her grade school, the same one I went to, little encouragement is given to write. I regretted my educational background from the moment I was assigned my first college paper.

– 7 –

Why did these white people know how to write so much better than I? Why did they go to the best schools while I went to run-down schools like Seward Park? Why didn't someone encourage me to write?

I would push Angelique as hard as I could. I would get her angry at the injustice around her, make her want to prove herself. If she learned to enjoy writing, I would be that much closer to making her a thinking person.

– 8 –

She wrote me like I asked her to, at first mostly drawing pictures and writing the standard "How are you doing" and "I miss you." Soon, however, her letters became more substantial. She wrote about the games she played in school, her new shoes, and why she still likes to watch *Ducktails*, even though her classmates say it's a baby cartoon.

– 9 –

do you love scary stoys? Well
you are going to loike this one
get wety here it is "HA" "HA" "HA" "HA"

   FRITE NIGHT FOR ANGELIQUE
It all started on Friday morning
It was 6 am I saw red drops from
my seling! Somehing is happing in
the adek I seid. I ran up the stars.
I herd a scem. I opened the door slowly
it was my mom. She was merded she was
stab. She is laing on the floor.
I scemed like I was going to die myself.
I called Chino. He came in a ower.
Every one we knew was dead. Some one was
kning on the door. It was the mertira.
I kict him in the nust. He drope the
gun and I pict up and seid if you toch
that rabbit your dead. He kick the rabbit.
I shot him in the hart thak his mask off
and it was Chino alalong.

– 10 –

I was proud of her. I liked her surprise ending — an unexpected twist.

She is learning to be a good writer. Is the ending a subconscious slip?

did I push her too hard?   No. After all, is it not I who plays
                             Barbie with her, who encourages
                             her and who thinks about what is
                             best for her? How could I be chok-
                             ing her?
I am sorry.   But I have to push hard.

– 11 –

That's What Siste'rs are for
And I neve thought I
felt this way
and I'm glad I got a chanse to say

that I do beleve I love you
and if I should ever go away
Well then close your eye
and trie
the thing we do today
and that if you can remmber
keep smiling, keep shing
Thrus me doling — thats
what sisters for.

– 12 –

Guilt

WRITING 1

Can you recall interpretive essays you have written in the past?
Describe your experience in writing one of these assignments,
successful or not.

WRITING 2

After reading "Angelique's Letter," freewrite for ten minutes about
your initial reaction to the text. You may want to consider how your
experience is similar to or different from Angel's and why.

EXPLORING A TOPIC

To develop an interpretation, you need to read a text carefully — and
more than once. The first time (or first few times) you read a text, you will be
reading to understand, sorting out what the text says on the literal level: who

is involved, where they are, what happens, how it all concludes. You need to move beyond this, however, to critical reading, in which you develop an understanding of the author's larger theme or purpose.

To do this, you will want to pay close attention to the text — every word the author chose, every thing he or she described (or left undescribed) is significant. It is important, though, to let your own ideas roam freely at this point. Don't try to force every last detail in the text into a tidy pattern; focus on questions, not answers. Freewriting, journal writing, clustering, outlining and annotating are helpful invention and discovery techniques at this stage.

Like a good issue for a position paper, a good topic for an interpretive essay must involve an interesting question that has more than one possible answer. Without the possibility of more than one answer, there is no debate, no argument, and no real interpretation. If the topic is not interesting, you will bore not only your readers but also yourself. Here are some suggestions for finding and exploring topics for interpretive essays.

Identify Questions, Problems, or Puzzles

Annotate the text with questions in the margins as you read the text or discuss it in class. Later you can explore each question to see if a suitable topic emerges. Good topics arise from material that is difficult to understand. Here, for example, are some of the questions that could be raised during a reading of "Angelique's Letter":

- Why does Angel Fuster focus so much on Angelique's writing?
- Why does he include the story about his own early sexual encounter in stanza 3?
- Why does Angelique identify Chino as the murderer in stanza 9?

Find Patterns of Repeated Words, Ideas, and Images

By repeating words, ideas, and images, writers call extra attention to them, often indicating that they are important to the meaning of the text. Often these patterns are strong enough to be called a theme — a major idea with which the work is concerned. For example, in "Angelique's Letter," the concepts of writing, race, sex, and guilt arise more than once.

Consider the Style, Organization, or Form

Careful writers try to make these elements contribute to the meaning of a text. As a critical reader you should try to decide why the writer made the choices he or she did. For example :

- Why does Fuster number his prose paragraphs as if they were poetic stanzas?

- Why does he arrange stanza 9 in opposite parallel columns?
- What is the effect of including Angelique's letters exactly as she wrote them?

Consider the Larger Context

You can often find an interesting topic by comparing the text with another, either one by the same author or a similar work by a different author. Carefully examine similarities and differences, looking for clues to why the author made the choices he or she did. For example, you could compare Fuster's essay with chapters in Mike Rose's *Lives on the Boundary* (1989) or with Julia Alvarez's *How the Garcia Girls Lost Their Accents* (1991), which also deal with growing up Hispanic in America. If the work you are interpreting has been published, consider reading what other reviewers or critics have said about it.

WRITING 3

Use at least three of the methods described in this section to find and explore potential topics for a text you are currently reading. Write journal entries, outlines, or rough notes about the possibilities, but do not, at this time, worry about developing your ideas thoroughly.

EXPLAINING A TEXT

Once you have explored several topics and settled on one, you will need to begin the task of explaining the text. You need to give your readers a grasp of the text as a whole, so that they can follow your interpretation as well as join in the act of interpreting themselves. This process is also valuable because it forces you to reexamine the details of the text.

Explanatory information in your essay should usually be written from an objective stance because you are focusing on the text, not yourself. Try to provide readers with all the information they will need to understand and evaluate your interpretation.

Identify and Summarize the Text

Your first job in writing about any text is to identify it thoroughly, yet briefly, so that readers know from the start what you are talking about. Identify its author, title, subject, and genre (what type of text it is — essay, poem, novel, and so on).

If the text tells a story, summarize the plot, character, and setting. If the text provides another kind of information (if it is, say, a poem or an argument), summarize the main ideas. In the following opening paragraph, Bob summarizes, "Angelique's Letter."

> "Angelique's Letter," an essay by Angel Fuster, explores one of the many struggles that minority families face in deteriorating inner cities throughout the country. Chino, the author and older brother, would like to see his nine-year-old sister, Angelique, rise above the lackluster education of her ghetto school. He does not want her to get pregnant and cut her education short as his mother and older sister did. Nor, however, does he want to stifle her with too much big brother advice.

Explain the Form and Organization

No matter what the text, some principle or plan holds it together and gives it structure. Texts that tell stories are often organized as a sequence or events in chronological order. Other texts may alternate between explanations and examples or between first-person and third-person narrative. You will have to decide which aspects of the text's form and organization are most important for your interpretation. Rebecca explains the unusual stanza organization of "Angelique's Letter":

> After Angelique's scary story, we see both sides of Angel's conscience in an argument made visible by writing it in two columns. On the left is the soft side of him who would like to praise her. On the right is the voice that wants to control and educate her. He concludes this section with "I don't know."

Describe the Author's Perspective

Describing the author's perspective provides your readers with clues about the author's theme and purpose, which will probably be important elements in your interpretation. In some cases, you will need to differentiate the author's perspective from those of the characters. In *The Color Purple*, for instance, novelist Alice Walker uses the voice of fourteen-year-old Celie as her narrator. "Angelique's Letter," however, is nonfiction, so Angel the author is the same person as the character his sister calls Chino. John attempts to describe Fuster's perspective:

> Angel writes as an angry but goal-driven older brother intent on protecting his sister from the destructive forces of the urban ghetto. At the same time, he views his attempt to save her as itself destructive. The resulting essay is more ironic and self-deprecating than angry and revolutionary.

Explain the Thesis or Theme

Tell your readers what the main point of the text is. In fiction, poetry, and reflective essays, the main point usually takes the form of an implicit

theme, while in most nonfiction it appears as a thesis, either stated or unstated. Remember that the theme or thesis of a text is different from your interpretation as a reader. A theme or thesis is what the text says it is about:
*"Angelique's Letter" is about the difficulties of growing up Hispanic and the obstacles
encountered by Hispanic youth in their attempts to make a better life for themselves
and their families.* An interpretation is the larger or deeper meaning that you, as
a critical reader, find in the story: *"Angelique's Letter" is about the author's uneasi-
ness with his well-educated self, which he fears has killed his neighborhood self.*

Place the Work in a Historical, Cultural, or Biographical Context

No text exists in isolation; it was created by a particular author in a particular place at a particular time. Describing this context provides readers with
important background information and indicates which conditions you think
were most influential. After learning more about the author through a personal
interview, Rebecca describes the circumstances that provide the background to
Fuster's essay:

> I particularly liked "Angelique's Letter" because it shows some of
> the experiences, anger, and frustration that nonwhite children, includ-
> ing Angel, faced growing up in the city. Angel drew on his own experi-
> ence of living in the Seward Park housing project on the Lower East
> Side of New York City.

WRITING 4

Look at the text you are now interpreting, and make brief notes
addressing each of the five elements described in this section.

TAKING A STAND

When you write an interpretation, you explain how a text works and
take a stand on what the text means, arguing from the most persuasive point
of view possible.

Understanding Interpretive Communities

The communities to which you belong shape who you are, how you see,
what you hear, and how you respond to the world. All of us belong to many
communities: families (parents and siblings, entire ethnic cultures), social and
economic groups (students or teachers, rich or poor), organizations (Brownies,
Boy Scouts, Democrats, Masons), neighborhoods (rural or urban, North or
South), and institutions (school, church, fraternity).

Those communities that influence you most strongly are your interpretive communities — they determine how you interpret the world. People who belong to the same community as you are likely to have similar assumptions and are therefore likely to interpret things as you would. People who belong to different communities are likely to have perspectives different from yours.

College is, of course, a large interpretive community. It is made up in turn of many smaller communities called disciplines — English, history, chemistry, business, and so on. To study a discipline for several semesters is to consciously adopt that community's way of looking at the world. Within any discipline are several established ways of interpreting texts. Within the field of English literature, for example, there are feminist critics and Marxist critics, scholars who rely heavily on biographical information about authors and those who look at only the words on the page.

When you take a stand in an interpretive essay, you will often do so from the perspective of a traditional academic interpretive community. Take care to follow the conventions and strategies of that community. Remember, though, that your view of the world is influenced by many other communities. Acknowledging these other communities — such as class, gender, race, family — and examining how they affect your reading can often lead to interesting insights and interpretations.

Choosing a Perspective

Many college assignments will ask that you interpret a text fairly, neutrally, and objectively — that you focus on the *object* (text) under study instead of the *subject* doing the study (yourself). This would seem to ask you to avoid showing any of those biases that inevitably come with your membership in various interpretive communities. Realistically, however, you can be objective only to a certain degree.

What such assignments really ask is that you adopt an objective stance, interpreting the text *as objectively as possible*, trying to see things as they exist apart from your preconceived way of viewing them. An objective stance is fair to the text, because you focus on the text itself without letting your feelings get in the way. Treating texts fairly and objectively — even those with which you strongly disagree — lays the foundation for strong and believable criticism: readers will be more willing to listen to your interpretations and evaluations if you have first demonstrated that you are unbiased.

When using an objective stance, write from the third-person point of view. Keep yourself and references to yourself out of your writing, and use language that is emotionally neutral and unbiased.

A few college assignments that call for interpretation will ask — or allow— you to take an admittedly subjective stance. Such assignments encourage you to acknowledge frankly the interpretive communities to which you belong. Instead of keeping your opinions or emotions out of the assignment, you incorporate them as it suits your purpose.

A subjective stance can be honest in admitting that complete objectivity is impossible. However, subjective writing sometimes becomes self-centered, with the writer digressing from the text into personal experience and opinion. The subjective stance is often distrusted in academic writing because it can divert attention from the object under study and misdirect it toward the writer.

When you write interpretive papers from a subjective stance, do so carefully. Use the first-person point of view, but not excessively or in every sentence. Refer to personal experience only when it supports your purpose. Make value judgments, but with care, caution, and respect for opposing opinions.

Some of the most accessible, readable, and honest interpretative writing is a mix of objective and subjective points of view: the writer focuses on the text and supports all assertions with evidence from the text, yet admits his or her own opinions and values at carefully selected points. Frequently, interpretive essays use an objective stance for explaining the text and a more subjective stance for interpreting it.

Developing and Supporting a Thesis

The thesis of your interpretive essay gives a clear, concise statement of your interpretation. It should answer the question that you identified as the topic of the paper.

QUESTION	Why does Angel Fuster focus so much on Angelique's writing?
THESIS	In "Angelique's Letter," Angel Fuster focuses on education and on writing in particular because he believes they will lead to a better life for Angelique and others like her.

Like an argumentative thesis, an interpretive thesis should answer an interesting question and should be focused enough that you can support it within the confines of your paper. Unlike an argumentative thesis, it does not propose a plan of action; rather, it proposes a way of seeing. A clear thesis not only helps readers understand what you are saying but also helps persuade them that your interpretation is careful and reasonable.

Stating your interpretation is one thing, persuading readers to believe it is another. You need to support your interpretation with examples from the text itself. To explore your topic and develop your thesis, you probably marked, collected, and copied passages from your reading. These passages will form the basis for your evidence. In addition, you may want to bring in other expert sources, such as those found through library research or interviews, to support your ideas.

When you draw on other sources to support your view, be careful how you bring that information into your text. You will need to decide when to summarize, when to paraphrase, and when to quote directly. Regardless of how you bring the outside information into your paper, remember that you must document each idea; to fail to do so is plagiarism. (For a complete explanation of using and documenting source material, see Chapter 19.)

WRITING 5

Write three possible statements about a text you are studying. Identify two quotations in the text that would support each statement. Conclude by freewriting about which thesis you would prefer to develop into a full-fledged interpretive essay.

SHAPING THE WHOLE PAPER

Angel Fuster's essay "Angelique's Letter" was read and interpreted by a class of first-year students. The assignment was in three parts. The first draft was to be an objective interpretation. The second draft was to be subjective, in the form of a personal letter to the author. And the third and final draft was to be a revision of whichever interpretation the student preferred. Two final drafts are reproduced here. The first is objective, the more common form of interpretive writing you will be asked to do in college. The second is subjective, a less common form of interpretive writing that is nonetheless powerful and important.

Objective Stance

Heather's essay "Slowing Down" is written from an objective stance. The writer is not present until the last paragraph, where Heather felt it necessary to step in personally and affirm her own feelings about Fuster's essay. Heather's organization follows Fuster's essay from beginning to end. Because she believes that Fuster's own words convey a great deal of power, she quotes him directly rather than paraphrasing or summarizing his text; notice that she integrates her quotes smoothly and grammatically with her own sentences.

Slowing Down

"Angelique's Letter" tells a story about how a Puerto Rican college student named Angel decides to see his nine-year-old sister Angelique grow up having pride in herself and her culture, despite the disadvantages she will have to face throughout her life because of her race and economic background. Understanding the importance of education and achievement, Angel sets out to instill in his sister a sense of value toward these things, hoping that will help her become all that she is capable of being.

The story begins with young Angelique displaying her excitement about learning. Using her newly acquired ability to write in script, she has written "Angelique" in her "fanciest style" on a sheet of blue-lined notebook paper. Looking for praise from her older brother, whom she calls by the family name Chino, she proudly displays her letter to him.

Rather than with praise and encouragement, however, Chino replies sarcastically, "like those restaurants only rich white people go to."

Chino's response is harsh, but he intends it to provoke thought and encourage his sister to become as angry as he is at the system that makes Puerto Ricans second-class citizens. However, Chino appears to worry about his own reaction, as he confesses to feeling "guilty for using her artistically written 'Angelique' to teach her about racism."

These first two passages are important in several ways. First, they show Chino's influence on his younger sister. Second, they introduce Chino's drive to make sure Angelique does not become pregnant and drop out of school "as many of her classmates will." Third, they show Chino's dedication to act on his resolve by turning innocent situations into lessons about inner-city life. Finally, the second passage ends with a clear warning that time is short, "and she was already talking about boys." If Chino wants to have an impact on his sister's life, he has to start now.

Chino's flashback about Sorada Rodriguez illustrates how little time he has to lose if he is going to make a difference in Angelique's life. Girls in this environment are forced to grow up very quickly. Chino has to prevent her from becoming too sexually active, like Sorada, at such a young age if she is to stay in school and do well.

Chino continues with his strategy to ensure that Angelique "grow into a thinking person." He shows how hard he will have to push, "using every opportunity . . . to bring up the subject." When Angelique offers him a blond Barbie, he replies, "No, I don't want her. I want the one with the black hair." So again he uses her simple game as a lesson in racial discrimination, and again he feels guilty, ending the episode with "I felt like telling her I was only kidding."

When Chino returns to school, Angelique writes to him as he has requested. He knows what it is like to grow up in a poor educational environment, since that is where he grew up too. Chino is still "bitter" because the other kids at college know how to write better, went to the best schools, and had the best teachers. But his bitterness leads him to push her too hard, too fast, as her scary story "Frite Night" makes clear to him; she has cast Chino in the role of the murderer. On the one hand, Chino is proud of the long imaginative story she has written, but on the other hand he wonders if he is "choking her." He ends his essay with the single word "Guilt"--his clear admission that, despite his good intentions, he is doing his sister wrong.

I do not pretend to understand the situation Chino and his sister are facing, so I really cannot judge whether Chino is right or wrong. His intentions are the best; however, I question whether instilling anger in a young child is a good thing to do. Anger is a powerful emotion, but it is also dangerous. There are other emotions, such as love, that encourage learning and self-improvement. Children need to be children, and childhood is the only time they can be that. There is nothing wrong with educating his sister, but, as Chino realizes himself by the end of his essay, he has to learn where and when to stop. If he does not stop, at least he knows he must slow down.

Subjective Stance

Pat takes a personal approach to finding meaning in Fuster's text, yet he supports his assertions in two important ways: first, by sharing relevant elements of his own experiences and, second, by quoting specific passages from Fuster's text that are important to him. While Pat's essay/letter is not analytic in a strict academic sense, it does analyze the text in light of his own experience.

Dear Angel,

I grew up in rural Vermont, a long way from places like Seward Park. My little town is surrounded by high mountains, not tall skyscrapers. But your paper made me think about Bethlehem, Pennsylvania, where I lived before my family moved to Vermont, nine years ago. We lived close to the projects, where both black and Hispanic families lived, and which my parents warned us to stay away from. I wonder what it is like now in my old neighborhood and what the future is of the people who live there. How many children have older brothers looking out for them, wanting them to grow up "questioning things"?

I learned a lot from "Angelique's Letter," not only about your life, but about mine as well. Though Angelique has formidable obstacles to overcome--especially since she is female--I learned that she has a powerful advocate in you, her older brother. You are a role model for her as well as for all of her friends who are trapped in that system. Your plan to make her a "thinking person" by writing letters is working, even though you worry about pushing her too hard. Remember that in addition to writing "Frite Night" she copied out the song "That's What Sisters Are For" and sent it to tell you she loved you. You have no choice; she does need to read, write, and become better educated to escape her life in the projects.

I also learned that I take my own educated life for granted. You "regretted [your] educational background from the moment [you were] assigned [your] first college paper." Well, compared to you, I have been handed everything on a silver platter, including a safe, comfortable, middle-class home, college prep classes, parents who nourished me, teachers who encouraged me. Reading and writing must have come easy to me since I seem to have been doing them all of my life.

What touches me most is your great concern for Angelique's future. Most people in your situation would be out for themselves and not thinking about what's best for the family they left behind. Instead you are trying to share your success with them, worrying, pushing, and keeping track of enough emotions for two people. Thank you for sharing your story with me.

Sincerely,

Pat

Strategies for Writing Interpretive Essays

1. Identify the text, your subject, and yourself fully and correctly.
2. State the thesis of your essay up front or lead up to it and state it at the end — but be sure to state it.
3. Use the third person (objective voice) in most interpretive writing. Use first person when you want to add relevant personal information or are writing deliberately from the subjective stance.
4. Write interpretive essays in a comfortable, semiformal style. Avoid both contractions and pretentiousness. Write in neutral, unemotional language that shows your interpretation to be careful and rational.
5. Provide a brief summary of what happens in the text, first to last, but keep your focus on *interpretation*, or what the text means.
6. When providing evidence for your assertions, quote directly to capture the special flavor of an author. Use summaries and paragraphs for other evidence.
7. Document any assertions not your own or any passages of text that you quote or paraphrase.

SUGGESTIONS FOR WRITING AND RESEARCH

Individual

1. Write the interpretive essay that you have been exploring in Writings 3–5. Write the first draft from an objective stance, withholding all personal judgments. Write the second draft from a subjective stance, including all relevant personal judgments. Write your final draft by carefully blending elements of your first and second drafts.
2. Locate at least two reviews of a current text (book, recording, exhibit) with which you are familiar, and analyze each to determine the author's critical perspective. Write your own review of the text, and agree or disagree with the approach of the reviewers you analyzed. If you have a campus newspaper, consider offering your review to the editor for publication.

44

Collaborative

As a class or small group, attend a local concert, play, or exhibition. Take good notes and, when you return home, write a review of this event that includes both an interpretation and a recommendation that readers attend it (or not).

Share these variations on the same theme with others in your class or group and explore the different judgments that arise as a result of different perspectives.

Chapter 7
Writing with Sources

I really don't mind doing the research. The library, once you get to know it, is a very friendly place. But when I go to write the paper I keep forgetting all the rules about what to quote, and what not to quote, and how to introduce quotations and not make them too long or too short. It seems like that part could be less confusing.

— JASON

LOCATING POTENTIAL SOURCES FOR A RESEARCH PROJECT IS ONE THING; deciding which ones to include, where to use them, and how to incorporate them is something else. Some writers begin making use of their sources in their very earliest explanatory drafts, perhaps by trying out a pithy quotation to see how it brings a paragraph into focus. Others prefer to wait until they have all or most of their note cards in neat stacks in front of them before making any decisions about what to include. No matter how you begin writing with sources, there comes a time when you need to incorporate them finally, smoothly, effectively, and correctly into your paper.

CONTROLLING YOUR RESOURCES

Once you've conducted some research and are ready to begin drafting, you need to decide which sources to use and how to use them. You can't make this decision based on how much work you spent finding and analyzing each source; you have to decide based on how useful the source is in answering your research question. In other words, you need to control your sources rather than letting them control you.

Papers written in an effort "to get everything in" are source-driven and all too often read like patch jobs of quotations loosely strung together. Your goal should be to remain the director of the research production, your ideas on center stage and your sources the supporting cast.

You may find that a potential source you decided not to take notes on has become crucial, while notes that initially seemed central are now irrelevant. Don't be discouraged. Real research about real questions is vital and dynamic, which means it's always changing. Just as you can't expect your first working thesis to be your final thesis, you can't expect to know in advance which sources are going to prove most fruitful. And, of course, you can collect more information once you've begun drafting. At each step in the process you see your research question and answer more clearly, so the research you conduct as you draft may be the most useful of all.

The best way to ensure that you and your thesis remain in control is to make an outline first and then organize your notes according to it. (If you compose your outline on a word processor, it will be easier to make changes later.) If you do it the other way around — organizing your notes in a logical sequence and then writing an outline based on the sequence — you'll be tempted to find a place for every note and to gloss over areas where you haven't done enough research. By outlining first, you let the logical flow of your ideas create a blueprint for your paper. (Of course, your outline may change as your ideas continue to develop.) If you can't outline before you write, then be sure to begin writing before you arrange your note cards.

Once you've outlined or begun drafting and have a good sense of the shape of your paper, take time to organize your notes. Set aside bibliographic and note cards for sources that you don't think you're going to use. Put the rest of the bibliographic cards in alphabetical order by the authors' last names and arrange your note cards so that they correspond to your outline. Integrate field research notes as best you can. Finally, you may want to go back to your outline and annotate it to indicate which source goes where. This will also show you if there are any ideas that need more research.

Keep in mind that referring more than two or three times to a single source — unless it is itself the focus of your paper — undercuts your credibility and suggests overreliance on a single point of view. If you find you need to refer often to one source, make sure that you have sufficient references to other sources as well.

WRITING 1

Describe your experiences writing research papers. Were there requirements for using a certain number or kind of sources? Did you or your sources control the paper?

WRITING 2

If you haven't already done so, use your research log to draft a tentative thesis and working outline for your research paper. Then arrange your note cards according to that working outline.

QUOTING, PARAPHRASING, AND SUMMARIZING

Once you know which sources you want to use in your paper, you still have to decide how to use them. The notes you made during your research are in many forms. For some sources, you will have copied down direct quotations; for others you will have paraphrased or summarized important information. For some field sources you may have made extensive notes on background information, such as your interview subject's appearance. For some library sources you may have photocopied whole pages, highlighting useful passages. Simply because you've quoted or paraphrased a particular source in your notes, however, doesn't mean you have to use a quotation or paraphrase from this source in your paper. Once again, you must remain in control. Make decisions about how to use sources based on your goals, not on the format of your research notes.

Whenever you quote, paraphrase, or summarize, you must acknowledge your source through documentation. Different disciplines have different conventions for documentation. The examples in this chapter use the documentation style of the Modern Language Association (MLA), the style preferred in the languages and literature. (See Chapter 20 for details about the MLA system as well as the American Psychological Association [APA] style used in the social sciences.)

Quoting

To quote a source, you use the writer's or speaker's own words, reproducing them exactly as they were in the original source.

Direct quotation provides strong evidence and can add both life and authenticity to your paper. However, too much quotation can make it seem as though you have little to say for yourself. Long quotations also slow readers down and often have the unintended effect of inviting them to skip over the quoted material. Unless the source quoted is itself the topic of the paper (as in a literary interpretation), limit brief quotations to no more than two per page and long quotations to no more than one every three or four pages.

Deciding When to Quote

Direct quotations should be reserved for cases in which you cannot express the ideas better yourself. Using only strong, memorable quotations will make your writing stronger and more memorable as well. Use them when the original words are especially precise, clear, powerful, or vivid.

Precise. Use direct quotations when the words are important in themselves or when they've been used to make fine but important distinctions.

Clear. Use quotations when they are the clearest statement available.

Powerful. Let people speak for themselves when their words are especially strong. Powerful words are memorable; they stay in the reader's mind long after the page is turned.

Vivid. Use direct quotation when the language is lively and colorful, when it reveals something of the author's or speaker's character and individuality.

Quoting Accurately and Effectively

To quote, you must use an author's or speaker's exact words. Slight changes in wording are permitted in certain cases but these must be clearly marked as your changes.

Although you can't change what a source says, you do have control over how much of it to use. Use only as long a quotation as you need to make your point. Remember that quotations should be used to support your points, not to introduce or make them. Be sure that when you shorten a quotation, you have not changed its meaning.

If you omit words within quotations for the sake of brevity, you must indicate that you have done so by using ellipsis points. Any changes or additions must be indicated with brackets.

ORIGINAL

The human communication environment has acquired biological complexity and planetary scale, but there are no scientists or activists monitoring it, theorizing about its health, or mounting campaigns to protect its resilience. Perhaps it's too new, too large to view as a whole, or too containing — we swim in a sea of information, in poet Gary Snyder's phrase. All the more reason to worry. New things have nastier surprises, big things are hard to change, and containing things are inescapable.

— STEWART BRAND, *The Media Lab*

INACCURATE QUOTATION

In The Media Lab, Steward Brand describes the control that is exerted by watchdog agencies over modern telecommunications: "The human communication environment . . ." (288).

By omitting certain words, the writer has changed the meaning of the original source.

INEFFECTIVE QUOTATION

In The Media Lab, Steward Brand notes that we have done little to monitor the growth of telecommunications. "Perhaps it's too new, too large to view as a whole, or too containing . . . All the more reason to worry. New things have nastier surprises, big things are hard to change, and containing things are inescapable" (288).

By quoting too much, the writer has allowed the quotation to introduce an important point rather than support it.

ACCURATE AND EFFECTIVE QUOTATION

In <u>The Media Lab</u>, Steward Brand notes that we have done little to monitor the growth of telecommunications. Modern communication technology may seem overwhelmingly new, big, and encompassing, but these are reasons for more vigilance, not less: "New things have nastier surprises, big things are hard to change, and containing things are inescapable" (258).

Integrating Quotations into Your Paper

Direct quotations are most effective when you integrate them smoothly into the flow of your paper. Readers should be able to follow your meaning easily and to see the relevance of the quotation immediately.

USING EMBEDDED OR BLOCK FORMAT. Brief quotations should be embedded in the main body of your text and enclosed in quotation marks. A brief quotation consists of four or fewer typed lines according to MLA style guidelines.

Photo editor Tom Brennan took ten minutes to sort through my images and then told me, "Most photography editors wouldn't take more than two minutes to look at a portfolio."

Longer quotations should be set off in block format. Begin a new line, indent ten spaces (for MLA), and do not use quotation marks.

Katie Kelly also focuses on Americans' peculiarly negative chauvinism, in this case the chauvinism of New York residents:

New Yorkers are a provincial lot. They wear their big city's accomplishments like blue ribbons. To anyone who will listen they boast of leading the world in everything from Mafia murders to porno moviehouses. They can also boast that their city produces more garbage than any other city in the world. (89)

INTRODUCING QUOTATIONS. Introduce all quoted material so that readers know who is speaking, what the quotation refers to, and where it is from. If the author or speaker is well known, it is especially useful to mention his or her name in an introductory signal phrase.

Henry David Thoreau asserts in <u>Walden</u>, "The mass of men lead lives of quiet desperation" (5).

If your paper focuses on written works, you can introduce a quotation with the title rather than the author's name, as long as the reference is clear.

> Walden sets forth one individual's antidote against the "lives of quiet desperation" led by the working class in mid-nineteenth-century America (Thoreau 5).

If neither the author nor the title of a written source is well known (or the speaker in a field source), introduce the quotation with a brief explanation to give your readers some context.

> Mary Catherine Bateson, daughter of anthropologist Margaret Mead, has become, in her own right, a student of modern civilization. In Composing a Life she writes, "The twentieth century has been called the century of the refugee because of the vast numbers of people uprooted by war and politics from their homes" (8).

EXPLAINING AND CLARIFYING QUOTATIONS. Sometimes you will need to explain a quotation in order to clarify why it is relevant and what it means in the context of your discussion.

> In A Sand County Almanac, Aldo Leopold invites modern urban readers to confront what they lose by living in the city: "There are two spiritual dangers in not owning a farm. One is the danger of supposing that breakfast comes from the grocery, and the other that heat comes from the furnace" (6). Leopold sees city dwellers as self-centered children, blissfully but dangerously unaware of how their basic needs are met.

You may also need to clarify what a word or reference within the quotation means. Do this by using square brackets.

> *UNCLEAR*
>
> Observing the remains of earwigs, sow bugs, moths, and spiders, Dillard reminds us that everything is changing, even in death: "Next week, if the other bodies are any indication, he will be shrunken and gray, webbed to the floor with dust."

> *CLEAR*
>
> Observing the remains of earwigs, sow bugs, moths, and spiders, Dillard reminds us that everything is changing, even in death: "Next week, if the other bodies are any indication, [the earwig] will be shrunken and gray, webbed to the floor with dust."

INTEGRATING QUOTATIONS GRAMMATICALLY. A passage containing a quotation must follow all the rules of grammatical sentence structure — tenses should be consistent, verbs and subjects should agree, and so on. If the form of the quotation doesn't quite fit the grammar of your own sentences, you can either quote less of the original source, change your sentences, or make a slight alterations in the quotation. Use this last option sparingly, and always indicate any change with brackets.

GRAMMATICALLY INCOMPATIBLE

If Thoreau thought that in his day, "The mass of men lead lives of quiet desperation" (Walden 5), what would he say of the masses today?

GRAMMATICALLY COMPATIBLE

If Thoreau thought that in his day, the "mass of men [led] lives of quiet desperation" (Walden 5), what would he say of the masses today?

GRAMMATICALLY COMPATIBLE

If Thoreau thought that in his day, the masses led "lives of quiet desperation" (Walden 5), what would he say of the masses today?

GRAMMATICALLY COMPATIBLE

In the nineteenth century, Thoreau stated, "The mass of men lead lives of quiet desperation" (Walden 5). What would he say of the masses today?

WRITING 3

Read through your research materials, highlighting any quotations you might want to incorporate directly into your paper. Use your research log to explore why you think these words should be quoted directly.

Paraphrasing

To paraphrase, you restate a source's ideas in your own words. The point of paraphrasing is to make the ideas clearer (both to your readers and to yourself) and to express the ideas in the way that best suits your purpose.

Deciding When to Paraphrase

In taking notes you may have written down or photocopied many quotations instead of taking the time to put an author's or speaker's ideas into your own words. As you draft, however, you should paraphrase or summarize most such information so that your paper doesn't turn into a string of undigested quotations.

Paraphrasing should generally re-create the original source's order, structure, and emphasis, and they should include most of its details. This means that a paraphrase is not usually much briefer than the original. Use paraphrases only when the original is already quite brief or when you need to present an author's or speaker's ideas in detail; otherwise, use a summary.

Paraphrasing Accurately and Effectively

Restate the source's ideas, but do so in your own words. You may need to rewrite a paraphrase several times in order to get it fully into your own voice. A paraphrase should say neither more nor less than the original source, and it should never distort the meaning of the source. The best way to make an accurate paraphrase is to stay close to the order and structure of the original passage and to reproduce its emphasis and details. However, don't use the same sentence patterns or vocabulary or you will risk inadvertently plagiarizing the source.

If the original source has used a well-established or technical term for a concept, you do not need to find a synonym for it. If you believe that the original source's exact words are the best possible expressions of some points, you may use brief direct quotations within your paraphrase, as long as you indicate these with quotation marks.

Keeping in mind the reason that you are including the source will help you decide how to paraphrase the ideas. Be careful, though, not to introduce your own comments or reflections in the middle of a paraphrase, unless you make it clear these are your thoughts, not the original author's or speaker's.

ORIGINAL

The human communication environment has acquired biological complexity and planetary scale, but there are no scientists or activists monitoring it, theorizing about its health, or mounting campaigns to protect its resilience. Perhaps it's too new, too large to view as a whole, or too containing — we swim in a sea of information, in poet Gary Snyder's phrase. All the more reason to worry. New things have nastier surprises, big things are hard to change, and containing things are inescapable.

— STEWART BRAND, *The Media Lab*

INACCURATE PARAPHRASE

In The Media Lab, Brand points out that the "communication environment" we live within is as complex and vast as any ecosystem on the planet. Yet no one monitors this environment, keeping track of its growth and warning us if something is about to go wrong. This is because the communication environment has become so large and all-encompassing in such a short time that we don't worry about it (258).

This paraphrase distorts the original passage by changing speculation ("perhaps") to assertion ("This is because").

ACCURATE PARAPHRASE

In The Media Lab, Brand points out that the "communication environment" we live within is as complex and vast as any ecosystem on the planet. Yet no one monitors this environment, keeping track of its growth and warning us if something is about to go wrong. This may be understandable, since the communication environment has become so large and all-encompassing in such a short time that we often overlook it. But this is exactly why we should worry: it's the very qualities of being recent, large, and all-encompassing that makes this environment potentially so dangerous (258).

WRITING 4

Read through your note cards for any passages you quoted directly from an original source. Find notes that now seem wordy, unclear, or longer than necessary for your purposes. Paraphrase any of these notes that you expect to use in your paper. Exchange your paraphrases and the originals with a classmate. Assess each other's work: Have you paraphrased the original source accurately? Have you used your own words and sentence structure to express the original idea?

Summarizing

To summarize, distill a source's words down to the main ideas and state these in your own words. A summary includes only the essentials of the original source, not the supporting details, and is consequently shorter than the original.

Deciding When to Summarize

Use summaries whenever your readers need to know only the main point that the original source makes, not the details of how the original makes this point.

You may have taken extensive notes on a particular article or observation only to discover in the course of drafting that all the detail you included is not necessary, given the correct focus of your paper. In such a case, you may be able to summarize your notes in a few sentences that effectively support your discussion.

Keep in mind that summaries are generalizations and that too many generalizations can make your writing vague and tedious. You should occasionally supplement your summaries with brief direct quotations or evocative details collected through observation in order to keep readers in touch with the original source.

Summarizing Accurately and Effectively

Summaries vary in length, and the length of the original source has no necessary relationship to the length of the summary you write. Depending on the focus of your paper, you may need to summarize an entire novel in a sentence or two, or you may need to summarize a brief journal article in two or three paragraphs. Remember that the more material you attempt to summarize in a short space, the more you will necessarily generalize and abstract it. Reduce a text as far as you can while still providing all the information your readers need to know. Be careful though, not to distort the original's meaning.

ORIGINAL

The human communication environment has acquired biological complexity and planetary scale, but there are no scientists or activists monitoring it, theorizing about its health, or mounting campaigns to protect its resilience. Perhaps it's too new, too large to view as a whole, or too containing — we swim in a sea of information, in poet Gary Snyder's phrase. All the more reason to worry. New things have nastier surprises, big things are hard to change, and containing things are inescapable.

— STEWART BRAND, *The Media Lab*

INACCURATE SUMMARY

The current telecommunications networks comprise a nasty, unchangeable, and inescapable environment (Brand 258).

ACCURATE SUMMARY

Steward Brand warns that we may soon regret not keeping a closer watch on the burgeoning telecommunications networks (258).

Guidelines for Using Quotation, Paraphrase, and Summary

Below are some rules of thumb to help you decide how to use sources in your paper.

QUOTATION

- To quote, use the author's or speaker's exact words.
- A quotation is the same length as in the source, although words may be omitted for brevity if the omission is indicated with ellipsis points.
- Use a quotation when the language of the original is particularly precise, clear, powerful, or vivid.

PARAPHRASE

- To paraphrase, put the author's or speaker's ideas in your own words.
- A paraphrase is about the same length as the passage in the source.
- Use a paraphrase when you need to include all or most of the details in the source.

SUMMARY

- To summarize, reduce the author's or speaker's ideas to the main points, and express these in your own words.
- A summary is shorter than the passage in the source.
- Use a summary when you need to include only the essential points in the source.

WRITING 5

Review your notes to find any sources on which you have taken particularly extensive notes. Would it be possible to condense these notes into a briefer summary of the entire work? Would it serve the purpose of your paper to do so? Why or why not?

USING DOCUMENTATION AND AVOIDING PLAGIARISM

Documentation is a systematic method for acknowledging sources. Documentation is important not only as an acknowledgment of indebtedness but also as a service to your readers and to later scholars. Knowledge in the academic community is cumulative, with one writer's work building on another's. After reading your paper, your readers may want to know more about a source you cited, perhaps in order to use it in papers of their own. Correct documentation helps these readers find the source quickly and easily. (See Chapter 20 for details of the MLA and APA styles.)

You do not need to document *common knowledge,* even if it is mentioned in or by your sources. Common knowledge is information that an educated person can be expected to know or any factual information that can be found in multiple sources. Examples include the dates of historical events, the names and locations of states and cities, the workings of political and economic systems, the general laws of science, and so on. However, when you read the work of authors who have specific opinions and interpretations of a piece of common knowledge and you use their opinions or interpretations in your paper, you need to give them credit through proper documentation.

Plagiarism is stealing ideas or information from somebody else and passing them off as your own. Whenever you introduce ideas or information from a source into your text, you need to cite the source for those ideas. Failing to cite a source is an unethical practice and at most colleges is grounds for discipline or even dismissal.

Not all plagiarism is intentional. Many writers are unaware of the guidelines for correctly indicating that they have borrowed words or ideas from someone else. Nevertheless, it is the writer's responsibility to learn these guidelines and follow them.

Keep in mind that when you paraphrase or summarize a source, you need to identify the author of those ideas just as surely as if you had quoted directly. The most common kind of inadvertent plagiarism is a paraphrase or summary of a source that stays too close to the writing or sentence structure of the original, sometimes including whole phrases from the original without quotation marks. To avoid plagiarism, use your own words to replace unimportant language in the original, place any particularly effective language within quotation marks, and be sure to cite the author and page number where you found the ideas in the source.

ORIGINAL

Notwithstanding the widely different opinions about Machiavelli's work and his personality there is at least one point in which we find a complete unanimity. All authors emphasize that Machiavelli is a "child of his age," that he is a typical witness to the Renaissance.

— ERNST CASSIER, *The Myth of the State*

PLAGIARIZED PARAPHRASE

Despite the widely different opinions about Machiavelli's work and personality, everyone agrees that he was a representative witness to the Renaissance (Cassier 43).

ACCEPTABLE PARAPHRASE

Although views on the work and personality of Machiavelli vary, everyone agrees that he was "a typical witness to the Renaissance" (Cassier 43).

Guidelines for Avoiding Plagiarism

1. When taking notes, include complete bibliographic or other source information for each note.
2. Enclose even short phrases borrowed from other sources within quotation marks.
3. Credit any paraphrased and summarized material as well as direct quotations.
4. Do not document common knowledge. Learn what is considered common knowledge within your community or the discipline within which you are writing your paper; if in doubt, ask your instructor.

WRITING 6

Read the following quotation from Mike Rose's *Lives on the Boundary*; then examine the three sentences that follow and explain why each is an example of plagiarism.

"The discourse of academics is marked by terms and expressions that represent an elaborate set of shared concepts and orientations; alienation, authoritarian personality, the social construction of self, determinism, hegemony, equilibrium, intentionality, recursion, reinforcement, and so on. This language weaves through so many lectures and textbooks, it is integral to so many learned discussions, that it is easy to forget what a forgein language it can be." (192)

1. The discourse of academics is marked by expressions that represent shared concepts.
2. Academic discourse is characterized by a particular set of coded words and ideas that are found throughout the college community.
3. Sometimes the talk of professors is as difficult for outsiders to understand as a forgein language is to a native speaker.

Chapter 8
Documenting Sources: MLA

E ACH DISCIPLINE HAS DEVELOPED its own conventions for documentation. The languages and literature use the style recommended by the Modern Language Association (MLA). Other fields in the humanities use a system of endnotes or footnotes. Social sciences use the style recommended by the American Psychological Association (APA). Natural sciences use the style recommended by the Council of Biology Editors (CBE) or a related style. You should use the documentation of the discipline for which you are writing; if you are in doubt, ask your instructor.

This chapter presents the most commonly used documentation system, the MLA.

MLA GUIDELINES

The Modern Language Association (MLA) system is the preferred form for documenting research sources in the languages and literature. The MLA system requires that all sources be briefly documented in text by an identifying name and page number (generally in parentheses) and that there be a Works Cited section at the end of the paper listing full publication information for each source cited. The MLA system is explained in detail in the *MLA Handbook for Writers of Research Papers*, 3rd ed. (New York: MLA, 1988), the book on which the information in this section is based.

Conventions for In-Text Citations

In-text citations identify ideas and information borrowed from other writers. They also refer readers to the end of the paper for complete publication information about each original source. The fields of languages and literature are not primarily concerned with when something was written but focus instead on writers and the internal qualities of texts. In-text citations of the MLA system therefore feature authors' names, book and article titles, and page numbers. The places and dates of publication are found only at the end in the Works Cited list. Following are some examples of how MLA in-text citation works. (See Chapter 21 for sample papers using this style of documentation.)

Single Work by One or More Authors

When you quote, paraphrase, or summarize the work of an author, you must include in the text of the paper the author's last name and the page or pages on which the original information appeared. Page numbers are inserted parenthetically, without the word *page* or abbreviation *p.* or *pp.*; authors' names may be mentioned in the text sentence or included parenthetically preceding the page number(s).

> Lewis Thomas notes that "some bacteria are only harmful to us if they make exotoxins" (76).

> In his 1974 book Lives of a Cell, Lewis Thomas explains simply and elegantly why bacteria endanger the human organism (74-79).

> We need only fear some bacteria "if they make exotoxins" (Thomas 76).

> Exotoxins make bacteria dangerous to humans (Thomas 76).

Note that a parenthetical reference at the end of a sentence comes before the period. There is no punctuation between the author's name and the page number(s).

If a work cited is by two or three authors, the text sentence or the parenthetical reference must include all the names: (Rombauer and Becker 715), (Child, Bertholle, and Beck 215). For works by more than three authors, you may list all the authors or, to avoid awkwardness, use the first author's name and add "et al." (Latin for "and others") without a comma: (Britton et al. 395).

Two or More Works by the Same Author

If your paper includes references to two or more works by the same author, your citation needs to distinguish the work to which you are referring. Either mention the title in your sentence or include a brief title in your parenthetical citation.

According to Lewis Thomas, "many bacteria only become dangerous if they manufacture exotoxins" (Lives 76).

"Many bacteria only become dangerous if they manufacture exotoxins" (Thomas, Lives 76).

Note that if a *parenthetical* citation includes both the author's name and a title, the two are separated by a comma; there is no comma between the title and the page number.

Unknown Author

When an author is unknown, as in some pamphlets, documents, and periodicals, identify the complete title in your sentence or include an abbreviated title in the parenthetical citation along with the page number.

According to Statistical Abstracts, the literary rate for Mexico stood at 75% for 1990, up 4% from census figures ten years earlier (374).

The government's ban on ivory even extends to piano keys, which now can be only plastic-coated ("Key Largo" 42).

Corporate or Organizational Author

When no author is listed for a work published by a corporation, organization, or association, indicate the entity's full title in the parenthetical reference: (Florida League of Women Voters 3).When such names are long, cite the organization in your sentence and put only the page number in parenthesis.

Authors with the Same Last Name

When you cite works by two or more authors with the same last name, include each author's first name either in your sentence or in the parenthetical citation: (Janice Clark 51).

Works in More than One Volume

When your sources include more than one volume of a multivolume work, indicate the pertinent volume number for each citation by placing it before the page number, followed by a colon and one space: (Hill 2: 70). If your sources include only one volume of a multivolume work, you need not specify the volume number in your in-text citation (you will specify it in your Works Cited list).

One-Page Works

When you cite a work that is only one page long (such as a newspaper or magazine article), it is not necessary to include the page number parenthetically. The author (or title if the author is unknown) is sufficient for readers to find the exact page number in your Works Cited list.

Quote from an Indirect Source

When a quotation or any information in your source is originally from another source, use the abbreviation "qtd. in."

> Lester Brown of Worldwatch feels that international agricultural production has reached its limit and that "we're going to be in trouble on the food front before this decade is out" (qt. in Mann 51).

Literary Works

In citing classic prose works that are available in various editions, provide additional information (such as chapter number or scene number) for readers who may be consulting a different edition. Use a semicolon to separate the page number of your source from this additional information: (331; bk. 10, ch. 5). In citing poems, use only line numbers, indicating that you are doing so by including the word *line* or *lines* in the first reference.

> In "The Mother," Gwendolyn Brooks remembers " . . . the children you got that you did not get, / The damp small pulps with a little or with no hair . . ." (lines 1-2). Later she recalls children that "never giggled or planned or cried" (30).

Cite verse plays using arabic numerals for act, scene, and line numbers, separated by periods: (*Hamlet* 4.4.31–39.)

More than One Work in a Citation

To cite more than one work in a single parenthetical reference, separate the references with semicolons: (Aronson, *Golden Shore* 177; Didion 49–50).

Long Quotation Set Off from Text

For quotations of four or more lines, which are set off from the text by indenting ten spaces, the parenthetical citation follows any end punctuation and is not followed by a period.

Conventions for Endnotes and Footnotes

MLA style allows notes only for comments, explanations, or information that cannot be accommodated in the text of the paper, for citation of several different sources, or for comments on sources. In general, omit such additional information unless it is necessary for clarification or justification of the text.

If notes are necessary, insert a raised (superscript) numeral at the reference point in the text; the note itself should be introduced by a corresponding raised numeral and indented.

TEXT WITH SUPERSCRIPT

The standard ingredients for guacamole include avocadoes, lemon juice, onion, tomatoes, coriander, salt, and pepper.[1] Hurtado's poem, however, gives this traditional dish a whole new twist (lines 10-17).

NOTE

[1]For variations see Beard 314, Egerton 197, Eckhardt 92, and Kafka 26. Beard's version, which includes olives and green peppers, is the most unusual.

Complete publication information for the references listed in the note would appear in the Works Cited list. Footnotes are placed, single-spaced, at the bottom of the page on which their text references appear. Endnotes are placed, double-spaced, on a separate page at the end of the paper (before the Works Cited), with the title *Note* or *Notes*. (For examples of format and use of endnotes, see Chapter 21.)

Conventions for Works Cited

All sources mentioned in a paper should be identified in a list of Works Cited at the end of the paper. The Works Cited list should follow specific rules for formatting and punctuation so that the reader can readily find information.

FORMAT. After the final page of the paper, title a separate page "Works Cited," an inch from the top of the page, centered, but not underlined and not in quotation marks. (If you are required to list all the works you have read in researching the topic, title the list "Works Consulted.") Number the page, following in sequence from the last page of your paper.

Double-space between the title and first entry. Begin each entry at the left margin and indent the second and subsequent lines of the entry five spaces. Double-space both between and within entries. If the list runs to more than a page, continue the page numbering in sequence but do not repeat the Works Cited title.

ORDER OF ENTRIES. Alphabetize your list of entries according to authors' last names. For entries by an unknown author, alphabetize according to the first word of the title (excluding an initial *A*, *An*, or *The*).

FORMAT FOR ENTRIES.   There are many variations on the following general formats to accommodate various kinds of sources. The following formats are the three most common.

GENERAL FORMAT FOR BOOKS

two spaces   two spaces
Author(s). Book Title. City of publication, with country or state postal
Indent 5   abbreviation if needed: Publisher, year of publication.
spaces   one space one space

GENERAL FORMAT FOR JOURNAL ARTICLES

two spaces   two spaces   one space   one space
Author(s). "Article Title." Journal Title volume number (year):
Indent 5   inclusive page numbers.   one space
spaces

GENERAL FORMAT FOR MAGAZINE AND NEWSPAPER ARTICLES

two spaces   two spaces   one space
Author(s). "Article Title." Publication Title date: inclusive page
Indent 5   numbers.   one space
spaces

PUNCTUATION.   In general, each major item of information (author, article or book title, edition, publication information) is followed by a period; such periods are followed by two spaces. For books, a colon separates the city from the publisher; for periodicals, a colon separates the date of publication from the page number(s). Commas separate multiple authors' names; commas also separate a book's publisher from the year of publication. The publication year of a journal is enclosed in parentheses.

AUTHORS.   The first author in an entry is listed last name first, followed by a comma and the first name or initial(s). For a work with more than one author, subsequent names are listed first name first. When more than one work is included by the same author, three hyphens are used for the name in entries after the first.

TITLES.   Titles and subtitles are listed in full. Capitalize the first, last, and all principal words. Underline the titles of books and periodicals; put quotation marks around the titles of essays, poems, articles, short stories, and so forth, that are part of a larger work.

PUBLISHERS.   Abbreviate publishers' names as discussed under "Abbreviations." If the title page indicates that a book is published under an imprint (for example, Arbor House is an imprint of William Morrow), list both imprint and publisher, separated by a hyphen (Arbor-Morrow).

DATES AND PAGE NUMBERS.   For books and journals, give only the year of publication. The year for books is followed by a period; the year for periodicals is within parentheses and is followed by a colon. For dates of weekly magazines and newspapers, use no commas to separate elements, and put the day before the month (25 Sept. 1954). For monthly magazines, give the month and the year, not separated by a comma. In the latter three cases, the date is followed by a colon.

Inclusive page numbers are separated by a hyphen with no space before or after (36-45); use all digits for second page numbers up to 99 and the last two digits only for numbers above 99 (130-38) unless the full sequence is needed for clarity (198-210). If subsequent pages do not follow consecutively (as is the case in a newspaper story), use a plus sign after the final consecutive page (39+, 52-55+).

ABBREVIATIONS.   In general, do not use state and country names with the city of publication. But when the state or country is necessary for clarity (to distinguish between Newark, NJ, and Newark, DE, for instance), use the post office abbreviations. Publishers' names are abbreviated by dropping the words *Press, Company,* and so forth ("Blair" for "Blair Press"); by using only the first in a series of names ("Farrar" for "Farrar, Straus & Giroux"); and by using only the last name of a person ("Abrams" for "Harry N. Abrams"). *University* and *Press* are abbreviated "U" and "P," with no periods (Columbia UP; U of Chicago P). All months except May, June, and July are abbreviated. For a book, if no publisher or date of publication is given, use the abbreviations "n.p." or "n.d."

Following are some examples of the Works Cited format for a variety of different sources. For sample Works Cited lists, see the first three papers in Chapter 21.

Documenting Books

Book by One Author

Thomas, Lewis. Lives of a Cell: Notes of a Biology Watcher. New York: Viking, 1974.

Book by Two or Three Authors

Fulwiler, Toby, and Alan Hayakawa. The Blair Handbook. Boston: Blair-Prentice, 1994.

Book by More than Three Authors

Britton, James, et al. The Development of Writing Abilities (11-18). London: Macmillan Education, 1975.

If there are more than three authors, you have the option of using the Latin abbreviation "et al." ("and others") or listing all authors' names in full as they appear on the title page.

Book by a Corporation, Association, or Organization

U.S. Coast Guard Auxiliary. Boating Skills and Seamanship.
Washington: Coast Guard Auxiliary National Board, 1988.

Alphabetize by the name of the organization.

Revised Edition of a Book

Hayakawa, S. I. Language in Thought and Action. 4th ed. New York:
Harcourt, 1978.

Edited Book

Hoy, Pat C., II, Esther H. Shor, and Robert DiYanni, eds. Women's
Voices: Visions and Perspectives. New York: McGraw, 1990.

Book with an Editor and Author

Britton, James. Prospect and Retrospect. Ed. Gordon Pradl. Upper
Montclair, NJ: Boynton, 1982.

Book in More than One Volume

Waldrep, Tom, ed. Writers on Writing. 2 vols. New York: Random,
1985-88.

When separate volumes were published in different years, include inclusive dates.

One Volume of a Multivolume Book

Waldrep, Tom, ed. Writers on Writing. Vol. 2. New York: Random,
1988.

When each volume has an individual title, list the volume's full publication information first, followed by series information (number of volumes, dates).

Churchill, Winston S. Triumph and Tragedy. Boston: Houghton, 1953.
Vol 6. of The Second World War. 6 vols. 1948-53.

Translated Book

Camus, Albert. The Stranger. Trans. Stuart Gilbert. New York:
Random, 1946.

Book in a Series

Magistrale, Anthony. Stephen King, The Second Decade: Danse
Macabre to The Dark Half. Twayne English Authors Ser. 599. New
York: Twayne-Macmillan, 1992.

Add series information after the title. Book titles within another title are not
underlined.

Reprinted Book

Hurston, Zora Neal. Their Eyes Were Watching God. 1937. New York:
Perennial-Harper, 1990.

Add the original publication date after the title; then cite the current edition
information.

Introduction, Preface, Foreword, or Afterword in a Book

Holroyd, Michael. Preface. The Naked Civil Servant. By Quentin
Crisp. New York: Plume-NAL, 1983.

Odell, Lee. Foreword. Writing across the Disciplines: Research into
Practice. Ed. Art Young and Toby Fulwiler. Upper Montclair, NJ:
Boynton, 1986.

Work in an Anthology or Chapter in an Edited Collection

Donne, John. "Tne Good-Morrow." The Metaphysical Poets. Ed. Helen
Gardner. Balitmore: Penguin, 1957. 58.
Gay, John. The Beggar's Opera. British Dramatists from Dryden to
Sheridan. Ed. George H. Nettleton and Arthur E. Case. Carbondale:
Southern Illinois UP, 1975. 530-65.
Lispector, Clarice. "The Departure of the Train." Trans. Alexis
Levitin. Latin American Writers: Thirty Stories. Ed. Gabriella
Ibieta. New York: St. Martin's, 1993. 245-58.

Enclose the title of the work in quotation marks unless the work was originally
published as a book, in which case underline it. At the end of the entry, add
inclusive page numbers for the selection. When citing two or more selections
from one anthology, list the anthology separately under the editor's name.

Selection entries will then need to include only a cross-reference to the anthology entry.

> Donne, John. "The Good-Morrow." Gardner 58.

Periodical Article Reprinted in a Collection

> Emig, Janet. "Writing as a Mode of Learning." College Composition
> and Communication 28 (1977): 122-28. Rpt. in The Web of
> Meaning. Ed. Janet Emig. Upper Montclair, NJ: Boynton, 1983.
> 123-31.

Include the full citation for the original periodical publication, followed by "Rpt. in" ("Reprinted in") and the book publication information. Give inclusive page numbers for both sources.

Article in a Reference Book

> "Behn, Aphra." The Concise Columbia Encyclopedia. 1983 ed.
> Miller, Peter L. "The Power of Flight." The Encyclopedia of Insects.
> Ed. Christopher O'Toole. New York: Facts on File, 1986. 18-19.

If the article is signed, begin with the author's name. For commonly known reference works, full publication information and editor's names are unnecessary. Page and volume numbers are unnecessary when entries are arranged alphabetically.

Anonymous Book

> The World Almanac and Book of Facts. New York: World Almanac-
> Pharos, 1993.

Alphabetize by title, excluding an initial *A*, *An*, or *The*.

Government Document

> United States. Central Intelligence Agency. National Basic Intelligence
> Fact Book. Washington: GPO, 1980.

If the author is identified, begin with that name. If not, begin with the government (country or state), followed by the agency or organization. The Government Printing Office is abbreviated GPO.

Dissertation

> Kitzhaber, Albert R. "Rhetoric in American Colleges." Diss. U of
> Washington, 1953.

Put the title in quotation marks. Include the university name and the year. For a published dissertation, underline the title and add publication information as for a book, including the order number if the publisher is University Microfilms International UMI.

Documenting Periodicals

Article, Story, or Poem in a Monthly or Bimonthly Magazine

Linn, Robert L., and Stephen B. Dunbar. "The Nation's Report Card
   Goes Home." <u>Phi Delta Kappan</u> Oct. 1990: 127-43.

Abbreviate all months except May, June, and July. Hyphenate months for bimonthlies (July-Aug. 1993). Do not list volume or issue numbers.

Article, Story, or Poem in a Weekly Magazine

Updike, John. "His Mother inside Him." <u>New Yorker</u> 20 Apr. 1992:
   34-36.

The publication date is inverted.

Article in a Daily Newspaper

Brody, Jane E. "Doctors Get Poor Marks for Nutrition Knowledge."
   <u>New York Times</u> 10 Feb. 1992, natl. ed.: B7.
"Redistricting Reconsidered." <u>Washington Post</u> 12 May 1992: B2.

If the article is unsigned, begin with its title. Give the name of the newspaper as it appears on the masthead, but drop any introductory *A, An,* or *The.* If the city is not in the name, it should follow the name in brackets: El Diario [Los Angeles]. Include with the page number the letter that designates a separately numbered section; if sections are numbered consecutively, list the section number (sec. 2) before the colon, preceded by a comma.

Article in a Journal Paginated by Volume

Harris, Joseph. "The Other Reader." <u>Journal of Advanced Composition</u>
   12 (1992): 34-36.

If page numbers are continuous from one issue to the next throughout the year, include only the volume number and year, not the issue number or month.

Article in a Journal Paginated by Issue

Tiffin, Helen. "Post-Colonialism, Post-Modernism, and the
   Rehabilitation of Post Colonial History." <u>Journal of Commonwealth</u>
   <u>Literature</u> 23.1 (1988): 169-81.

If each issue begins with page 1, include the volume number followed by a period and the issue number. Do not include the month of publication.

Editorial

> "Price Support Goes South." Editorial. Burlington Free Press 5 June 1990: A10.

If signed, list the author's name first.

Letter to the Editor and Reply

> Kempthorne, Charles. Letter. Kansas City Star 26 July 1992: A16.
> Massing, Michael. Reply to letter of Peter Dale Scott. New York Review of Books 4 Mar. 1993: 57.

Review

> Rev. of Bone, by Faye Myenne Ng. New Yorker 8 Feb. 1992: 113.
> Kramer, Mimi. "Victims." Rev. of 'Tis Pity She's a Whore. New York Shakespeare Festival. New Yorker 20 Apr. 1992: 78-79.

If a review is unsigned and untitled, begin the entry "Rev. of"; alphabetize by the name of the work reviewed. If the review is unsigned but titled, begin with the title. If the review is of a performance, add pertinent descriptive information such as director, composer, or major performers.

Documenting Other Sources

Pamphlet

Cite as you would a book.

Cartoon

> Roberts, Victoria. Cartoon. New Yorker 13 July 1992: 34.
> MacNelly, Jeff. "Shoe." Cartoon. Florida Today [Melbourne] 13 June 1993: 8D.

Computer Software

> Fastfile. Computer software. Computerworks, 1992. MS-DOS, disk.

List title first if the author is unknown. Name the distributor and the year published. List other specifications (such as the operating system, the units of memory, and the computer on which the program can be used) as helpful.

Film or Videocassette

Casablanca. Dir. Michael Curtiz. With Humphrey Bogart and Ingrid
    Bergman. Warner Bros., 1942.

Begin with the title followed by the director, the studio, and the year released.
Including the names of lead actors and other personnel following the director's
name is optional. If your essay is concerned with a particular person's work on
a film, lead with that person's name.

Lewis, Joseph H., dir. Gun Crazy. Screenplay by Dalton Trumbo. King
    Bros., 1950.

Personal Interview

Holden, James. Personal interview. 12 Jan. 1993.
Morser, John. Professor of Political Science, U of Wisconsin.
    Telephone interview. 15 Dec. 1993.

Begin with the interviewee's name, and specify the kind of interview and the
date. Identify the individual's position if it is important to the purpose of the
interview.

Published or Broadcast Interview

Steinglass, David. Interview. Counterpoint. 7 May 1970: 3-4.
Lee, Spike. Interview. Tony Brown's Journal. PBS. WPBT, Miami.
    20 Feb. 1993.

Begin with the interviewee's name. Include appropriate publication information for a periodical or book, and appropriate broadcast information for a radio or television program.

Unpublished Lecture, Public Address, or Speech

Graves, Donald. "When Bad Things Happen to Good Ideas." NCTE
    Convention. St. Louis, 21 Nov. 1989.

Begin with the speaker, followed by the title of the address (if any), the meeting (and sponsoring organization if needed), the location, and date. If untitled,
use a descriptive label (such as *Speech*) with no quotation marks.

Personal or Unpublished Letter

Friedman, Paul. Letter to the author. 18 Mar. 1992.

Begin with the name of the letter writer, and specify the letter's audience.
Include the date written if known, the date received if not. To cite an unpub-

lished letter from an archive or private collection, include information that locates the holding (for example, "Quinn-Adams Papers. Lexington Historical Society. Lexington, KY").

Published Letter

Smith, Malcolm. "Letter to Susan." 15 Apr. 1974. The Collected
    Letters of Malcolm Smith. Ed. Sarah Smith. Los Angeles:
    Motorcycle, 1989. 23.

Cite a published letter like a selection from an anthology. Specify the audience in the letter title. Include the date of the letter immediately following its title. Also include the page number(s) following the publishing information. In citing more than one letter from a collection, cite only the entire work and list dates and individual page numbers in the text.

Map

Northwest United States. Map. Seattle: Maps Unlimited, 1978.

Cite as you would a book by an unknown author. Underline the title and identify it as a map or chart.

Performance

Rumors. By Neil Simon. Dir. Gene Saks. Broadhurst Theater, New
    York. 17 Nov. 1988.
Bissex, Rachel. Folk Songs. Flynn Theater, Burlington, VT. 14 May
    1990.

Identify the pertinent details such as title, place, and date of performance. If you focus on a particular person (such as the director or conductor), lead with that person's name. For a recital or individual concert, lead with the performer's name.

Recording

Marley, Bob, and the Wailers. "Buffalo Soldier." Legend. Island
    Records, 422 846 210-4, 1984.
Mahler, Gustav. Symphony no. 5. Compact disc. Cond. Seiji Ozawa.
    Boston Symphony Orch. Philips, 432 141-2, 1991.

Depending on the focus of your essay, begin with the artist, composer, or conductor. Enclose song titles in quotation marks, followed by the recording title underlined. (Do not underline musical compositions identified only by form, number, and key.) Specify the recording format for a tape or compact disc. End with the company label, the catalog number, and the date of issue.

Television or Radio Program

"Emissary." Star Trek: Deep Space Nine. Teleplay by Michael Pillar.
Story by Rick Berman and Michael Pillar. Dir. David Carson. Fox.
WFLX, West Palm Beach. 9 Jan. 1993.

If the program is not an episode of a series or the episode is untitled, begin with the program title. Include the network, the station and city, and the date of broadcast. Including other information (such as narrator, writer, director, performers) depends on the purpose of your citation.

Work of Art

McIntyre, Linda. Colors. Art Inst. of Chicago.
Holbein, Hans. Portrait of Erasmus. The Louvre, Paris. P. 148 in The
Louvre Museum. By Germain Bazin. New York: Abrams, n.d.

Begin with the artist's name. Follow with the title, and conclude with the location. If your source is a book, give pertinent publication information.

Documenting More than One Source by the Same Author

Subsequent Source by the Same Author

Thomas, Lewis. Lives of a Cell: Notes of a Biology Watcher. New York:
Viking, 1974.
---. The Medusa and the Snail: More Notes of a Biology Watcher. New
York: Viking, 1979.

The three hyphens stand for the same name (or names) in the previous publication.

Handout: Photocopy, Mimeograph, or Unpublished Paper

Clarke, John. "Issue Tree." Handout, History of Education, U of
Vermont, 1983.

Illustration: Drawing, Photograph, or Transparency

"Vital Statistics." Chart. Car and Driver Aug. 1992: 74.

If your essay deals, for example, with the work of a particular photographer, you should lead with the creator's name. Otherwise, lead with the title, or, if untitled, lead with the identifying label without quotation marks.

Chapter 9
How Writers Revise

Writing. I'm more involved in it. But not as attached. I used to really
cling to my writing, and didn't want it to change. Now I can see
the usefulness of change. I just really like my third draft, but I
have to let it go. But that's not what it's all about. I can still really
enjoy my third draft and still create another exciting paper.

– KAREN

A FIRST DRAFT IS A WRITER'S FIRST ATTEMPT TO GIVE SHAPE TO AN IDEA, argument, or experience. Occasionally, this initial draft is just right and the writing is done. More often, however, the first draft shows a broad outline or general direction that needs further thinking, further revision. An unfocused first draft, in other words, is not a mistake, but a start toward a next, more focused draft.

No matter how much prior thought writers give to complex composing tasks, once they begin writing, the draft begins to shift, change, and develop in unexpected ways. In other words, the act of writing itself produces new questions and insights that must be dealt with and incorporated into the emerging piece of writing. That's where active and aggressive revision strategies can help.

For many novice writers, revising is an alien activity that neither makes sense nor comes easy. Experienced writers, though, know that revising is the very essence of writing, the primary way of developing thoughts and preparing them to be shared with others. The rest of this chapter introduces strategies and procedures for effective revision.

UNDERSTANDING REVISION

Revising, editing, and *proofreading* are sometimes used to mean the same thing, but there is a good reason to understand each as a separate process, each in its own way contributing to the production of good writing. When you *revise,* you reread, rethink, and reconstruct your thoughts on paper until they match those in your mind. Revising is, literally, reseeing your focus, thesis, ar-

76

gument, evidence, arrangement, and conclusion and making major changes that affect the content, direction, and meaning of your paper. Revising generally takes place at the paragraph level.

When you *edit*, you change your language more than your ideas. After you know what you want to say and have written it, you edit by testing each word or phrase to see if it is necessary, accurate, and correct and if it conveys your intended tone and style. Editing takes place at the level of the sentence or word. The many dimensions of editing, including proofreading, are treated in Part VII.

When you *proofread*, you check very specific sentence elements for correctness: mainly spelling, punctuation, and capitalization. Proofreading is the final stage of the editing process, so it makes most sense to do it at the very end, when you have addressed style and grammar and simply want to make sure your paper contains no errors to distract or confuse readers.

There are two good reasons to revise before you edit. First, when you revise you may cut out whole sections of a draft because they no longer suit your final purpose. If you have already edited those sections, all your careful sentence-level work goes for naught. Second, if you've invested time in carefully editing sentences, you may be reluctant to cut them — even though cutting may make your paper better. Of course, writers are always circling back through the stages, mixing them up, editing after drafting, revising as they invent, drafting new paragraphs when they intend only to edit. Nonetheless, your work will probably be more productive (and you will probably be happier) if you resist as much as possible the urge to edit before you revise.

Revision is a complex and dynamic process. Exactly how to approach it is up to you, of course, but you may want to take advantage of some of the tried-and-true revision strategies described here. These will guide you in thinking profitably about revising and will ensure that your revising is thorough and appropriate.

WRITING 1

Describe one paper that you spent a long time revising. What was the assignment? How did you approach it? Did you plan to revise or did you just fall into the process? How many drafts did you write? Can you single out when you "drafted," when you "revised," and when you "edited"? What was the result of your revision work? Were you pleased? Was your audience?

ASKING REVISION QUESTIONS

Learning to revise means learning to ask careful questions about the purpose of your text, the audience for whom it's intended, and yourself as its author. The answers to these questions will help you decide what aspect of your paper to change when revising.

Ask Questions About Your Purpose

Revising is your last opportunity to modify your paper's purpose. While it's important to think about purpose when planning and drafting a paper, it's crucial to get the purpose straight when you revise. In fact, it's often easier to see your purpose — or lack thereof — most clearly after you have written a draft or two. Expect to return to the basic questions about purpose that you asked during planning (see Chapter 4):

1. Why am I writing this paper?
2. Do all elements and parts of the paper advance this purpose? If not, why not?
3. What was the assignment? Does my paper fulfill the assignment's requirements?
4. What is the aim of the paper? To narrate, explain, interpret, argue, reflect, or something else? Will my readers be able to tell that this is what I'm doing?
5. What is my theme or thesis? Have I expressed it clearly?

Ask Questions About Your Audience

You also need to make sure your paper is aimed accurately at your audience. If in planning and drafting you have been most concerned with gathering information and putting your ideas together in a coherent manner, at some point you need to switch your attention to your audience, asking questions like these:

1. Who is my audience for this paper?
2. What do my readers know about this subject? Have I told them too much that they already know?
3. What do my readers not know about this subject? Have I given them the context they need?
4. What questions or objections do I anticipate my audience raising? Can I answer any of them before they are asked?
5. Are my tone and style appropriate to this audience?

For more information on writing to specific audiences, see Chapter 5.

Ask Questions About Yourself

Perhaps the best reason for revising is to know for yourself that you have written the best paper possible. Revise so that when you read the paper you enjoy both its ideas and its language. If you are writing from personal experience, make that experience ring true; if you are writing an argument, develop one you believe in. When you please and convince yourself, you improve your chances of pleasing and convincing others as well. Ask questions like these:

1. Do I believe everything I've written in this paper? If not, why not?

2. What doubts do I have about my paper? Can I still address these?
3. Which passages do I most enjoy reading? How can I make the rest of the paper more like them?
4. Which passages do I find difficult to read? What can I do to change them?

USING REVISION STRATEGIES

This section lists more than a dozen time-tested revision strategies that may be useful to you. While they won't all work for you all the time, some will be useful at one time or another. Notice that these suggestions start with larger concerns and progress toward smaller ones.

Plan for Revising

You cannot revise if your haven't first written. If you are used to writing papers the day or night before they are due, you will not leave yourself time for revising. Plan from the outset to write early and to make time for all subsequent stages of the writing process, including revising.

Keep a Revision Notebook

If you regularly keep a journal, you can use it to write about revision plans. If you don't already keep one, you might consider using a portion of your class notebook for revision ideas. Be sure to record notes about books or articles related to your project as well as ideas about theme, direction, and purpose. Making time to write about your writing may contribute in surprising ways to the writing itself. (See Chapter 8 for further suggestions about keeping a journal.)

Impose Due Dates

After you write the due date for the final draft in your calendar or appointment book, add self-imposed due dates for revising and editing. Leave yourself time to return to your draft before your instructor's due date.

Establish Distance

The most important condition for revising well is to gain some distance from your first-draft thoughts. Even letting a draft sit overnight and then returning to it the next day allows you to see it differently — more objectively, more clearly. When you reread the whole piece, you'll almost always see places that satisfied you yesterday, but now, by the light of a new day, don't. Allow time to expect this possibility rather than dread it.

You can also achieve distance by typing rather than handwriting drafts and by asking others to read your paper with fresh eyes and without your preconceptions.

Type All Drafts

Handwriting can be too friendly, too familiar to allow you to see your thoughts clearly. As soon as you can, type your thoughts so you can look at them on a computer screen or piece of paper. Seeing your thoughts may make it easier to change, expand, or delete them. Typing drafts on a computer will also encourage revising and editing, since you can change your words, phrases, and sentences without retyping every one.

Request Response

It always helps to share a draft of your paper with readers you trust. No matter how good a writer you are or how good you feel about a particular paper, getting another opinion will give you new ideas. When you ask for a response, be sure to specify what kind of response you want. In an early draft, for instance, you might request a response to your larger ideas; in a later draft, you might request more attention to matters of tone, style, or detail; in a final draft you may simply want help with proofreading.

Reconsider Everything

When you return to your draft for revision, reread and reconsider the whole text. First, reconsider it in light of the assignment: Does the paper address the question it was supposed to address? Next, reread the whole paper from the start; every time you change something of substance, reread the whole thing again. Remember that revision is conceptual work in which you try to get your thoughts just right and in the right order. If you change the information on one page, you may need to change ideas, questions, or conclusions on another page. Finally, if a classmate or instructor has made comments on some parts of the paper and not on others, do not assume that those are the only places where revision is needed.

Believe and Doubt

Reread your draft as a believer (imagine a supportive friend), putting checks in the margins next to passages that are most convincing — the assertions, the dialogue, the details, the evidence. Then reread the draft as a skeptic (imagine your most critical teacher), putting question marks next to all passages that seem questionable. Finally, review the paper, being satisfied at the check marks that assure you the paper is on the right track and answering the doubts raised by the question marks.

Test Your Theme or Thesis

Sometimes while revising, you generate new ideas, raise new questions, add and subtract information, and end up with a theme or thesis quite different from the one you set out to demonstrate. Consequently, it's a good idea whenever you revise to return periodically to your thesis to make sure it still corresponds to what you've actually written. If not, you can either realign your paper, making it conform to the theme or thesis you originally envisioned, or change the theme or thesis to reflect the content of your paper.

Evaluate Your Evidence

To make any theme or thesis convincing, you need to support it with evidence. Check to see if your evidence, examples, and illustrations provide that support. Ask the following questions:

- Do the evidence and examples support my thesis or advance my theme?
- What objections can be raised about my evidence?
- What additional evidence will answer these objections?

Make a Paragraph Outline

Each paragraph in your paper should be a group of sentences focused on the same main idea. The whole paper is a series of such paragraphs. A paragraph outline at the revision stage creates a map of your whole paper and lets you see where organization is effective and changes need to be made. To make a paragraph outline, number each paragraph and write a phrase describing its main idea. When you are finished you can see whether adjacent paragraphs develop your overall topic or theme in a logical manner. If not, you can reorganize them first in the outline and then in the paper itself. A word processor makes it especially easy to make an outline and then move items around until they fit most logically. (For more information on paragraphs, see Chapter 26.)

Limit and Cut

Professional writers often use revision to cut out, delete, and simplify their writing; in writing as in living, less is often more. When you revise, eliminate all passages that do not contribute necessary information to the point you want your paper to make. This is especially important when you have collected a lot of research information and try to make it all fit into your paper; information that doesn't fit confuses readers more than it impresses them. (For more information on limiting and cutting, see Chapter 23.)

Add and Amplify

Sometimes even as you limit and cut your text, you may also need to expand on some ideas. When you revise, keep asking yourself whether you have explained every concept clearly and added the information, illustrations, and examples to make your paper convincing. (For more information on adding and amplifying, see Chapter 23.)

Switch and Transform

Reconsider your existing draft in light of new possibilities: What would happen if you switched the tense in which it is written or the point of view from which it is told? What would happen if you recast it into a different form? Look at your current draft and ask whether it could communicate even better if you switched or transformed the material. (For more information on switching and transforming, see Chapter 24.)

Listen for Your Voice

When your paper is nearly finished, read it out loud and see if it sounds like you talking. In many informal and semiformal papers, your language should sound like you, a real human being, speaking. If it doesn't, you should attempt to revise it so that it does. In more formal papers, such as science and research reports, the language should not sound like you talking; if it does, revise to make it less personal and more objective. And in some papers, you may want different sections to sound like different voices speaking. Keep in mind that while the complex concept of voice includes tone and style, it includes the writer's values and choices, and what he or she stands for. Ask these questions about your voice:

- Where do I hear or see evidence of my voice: in which words, phrases, sentences, or paragraphs?
- What does my voice sound like: confident, questioning, diplomatic, uncertain, arrogant, friendly, or humorous?
- What do I want to sound like?

Let Go

The spirit of revision is the welcome acceptance of change, the belief that no matter how good something is, it can always be made better. But many writers become attached to their words, proud to have generated so many of them in the first place, reluctant to abandon them once generated. When writers learn to let go, they have learned to trust that their power, creativity, and authority can generate exciting writing again and again, on demand. Letting go can imply dropping whole sections or even whole drafts.

Consider revising by starting a completely new second draft. After you have written and reread your first draft, start a new one as if you no longer have a written draft to tinker with. Sometimes your best writing will result from a new start on old material as you automatically delete and edit out dead-end ideas and are not constrained from finding better ones. This approach is especially easy if you are writing on a computer. You can make a new file for the new draft and keep the old one in a backup file just in case you change your mind.

> **WRITING 2**
>
> Return to an early draft of a paper you are writing and examine it in light of the strategies suggested in this section. Which suggestions proved most useful? Do you know why?

REVISING WITH A COMPUTER

A computer can make every stage in your writing process easier and can help you improve many aspects of your writing. In addition, it can make writing more fun. Word processing programs have virtually revolutionized how writers work, allowing them to draft, revise, experiment, reshape, and edit any number of times before committing to a final draft. And they can catch and correct spelling mistakes in the final draft.

It really doesn't matter what brand of computer you use, whether you own it or not, which word processing program you have, or what kind of disk your computer is equipped with. A computer aids revision in numerous ways.

A computer makes it easier to move back and forth in your text as you revise. It facilitates the typical nonlinear writing process in which you may jump around from planning to drafting to researching to revising, keeping everything fluid until you call it finished.

A computer offers distinct advantages at each stage in your writing: when looking for ideas, the computer makes everything — from freewriting to list-making and outlining — fluid, flexible, and instantly changeable — as early draft plans need to be. When you're drafting and revising, the computer stores text and so makes it, at the same time, changeable, moveable, and recoverable. When you're editing, it allows you to easily rearrange words. A computer also makes it easy to add new research; some software programs provide on-line help and automatic formatting with documentation conventions.

A computer can help create the distance you need for effective revising. As they appear on a computer screen or as printed in good-looking type on fresh sheets of paper, your ideas may be easier to reread with detachment. Be careful, though: a good-looking typeface may make your thoughts look more professional and profound than they may really be; don't be lulled into complacency just because the type looks good.

If you need to add details or supporting evidence, a computer can help you find new information easily and quickly. When equipped with a *modem*, your computer can gain access to library information from your home or dorm. Instead of traveling physically to locate books, periodicals, and special collections, you can search for and often even print out some information from sources within the library. In addition, you can share your drafts with other writers via electronic mail, sending text and comments back and forth.

Sophisticated and powerful software can help you improve your final draft by checking your spelling, grammar, and style.

And of course, when you're finished revising and editing, you can produce a professional-looking, visually exciting paper using the computer's fonts and graphics capabilities. Keep in mind, however, that fancy fonts and graphics are no substitute for clear language, logic, and organization.

WRITING 3

If you currently write on a computer, explain the major advantage of this writing tool. If you do not write with a computer yet, make a resolution to get thee to a computer lab on campus and learn.

Review to Revise

1. Reread the *assignment* and state it in your own words. Does your first draft adequately address the assignment?
2. Advance your *purpose*. Draw a vertical line in the margin next to passages that most clearly advance your purpose; plan to return to these and make them even stronger.
3. Question your *purpose*. Place a question mark in the margin next to passages that do not clearly advance your purpose and consider eliminating or rewriting them.
4. Describe your *audience*. What do they already know or assume? What context or background do they need? On what points do they already agree with you? On what points will you need to persuade them?
5. Underline the sharpest statement of *thesis* or *theme* in your paper. Do you have such a statement? Should you? Where is it located? Can it be made stronger?
6. Put a check mark next to each specific paragraph that contains *evidence* to support your thesis or theme. Do you introduce your strongest evidence first or last? Can you think of other examples, illustrations, or quotations that would provide more or stronger evidence?
7. *Outline* the paper, paragraph by paragraph. Is it clear which paragraphs contain *coordinate* ideas? Are these supported by paragraphs that contain *subordinate* ideas?
8. Read your paper *out loud* and see if you believe it and like it.

SUGGESTIONS FOR WRITING AND RESEARCH

1. Select any paper that you wrote and considered finished in one draft but that you believe would profit from revision. Revise the paper by using some of the revision strategies suggested in this chapter.

2. Go to the library and research the revision habits of a favorite or famous writer. If you cannot find such information, interview a professor, teacher, or other person on your campus or in your community who writes and publishes frequently. Find out about the revision process he or she most often uses. Write a report explaining the concept of revision as understood and used by a professional writer.

Chapter 10
Working Paragraphs

Paragraphs tell readers how writers want to be read.
— WILLIAM BLAKE

WHILE THERE ARE NO HARD AND FAST RULES FOR EDITING, there are important points to keep in mind as your essay nears completion. Once you are satisfied with the general shape, scope, and content of your paper, it's time to stop making larger conceptual changes — to stop revising — and start attending to smaller changes in paragraphs, sentences and words — to begin editing. When you edit, you shape these three elements (paragraphs, sentences, and words) so that they fulfill the purpose of the paper, address the audience, and speak in the voice you have determined is appropriate for the paper.

This chapter describes the way in which you design and shape effective paragraphs. Chapter 26 examines the specialized paragraphs that open and close your paper. And Chapter 27 shows you how to put together sentences and choose words for maximum effect.

THE WORK OF PARAGRAPHS

Most texts of a page or more in length are subdivided by indentations or breaks — paragraphs — that serve as guideposts, or as Blake puts it, "that tell readers how writers want to be read." Readers expect paragraph breaks to signal new ideas or directions; they expect each paragraph to have a single focus as well and to be organized in a sensible way; and they expect clear transition markers to link one paragraph to the next.

In truth, however, there are no hard and fast rules for what makes a paragraph, how it needs to be organized, what it should contain, or how long it should be.

I could, for instance, start a new paragraph here (as I have just done), leaving the previous sentence to stand as a single-sentence paragraph and so call a little extra attention to it. Or I could connect both that sentence and these to the previous paragraph and have a single five-sentence paragraph to open this section.

Most experienced writers paragraph intuitively rather than analytically; that is, they indent almost unconsciously, without thinking deliberately about it, as they develop or emphasize ideas. Sometimes their paragraphs fulfill conventional expectations, presenting a single well-organized and -developed idea, and sometimes they serve other purposes — for example, creating pauses or breathing spaces or points of emphasis.

The example paragraphs that follow are excerpts from student papers that have already appeared in this textbook. The paragraphs do different kinds of work, and although each is a good example, none is perfect. As you study them, bear in mind that each is illustrative of various purposes and organization, not definitive.

WRITING WELL-ORGANIZED PARAGRAPHS

Unity: Stick to a Single Idea

Paragraphs are easiest to write and easiest to read when each one presents a single idea, as most of the paragraphs in this textbook do. The following paragraph, from Brendan's essay on reintroducing wolves to Yellowstone National Park, focuses strictly on the role of wolves in the park.

> In recent years there has been a movement to bring the wolf back to Yellowstone Park. A battle is being waged between environmental conservationists, who support the reintroduction of wolves, and sheep and cattle farmers and western hunters, who oppose it. So far, legislators, representing the farmers and hunters, have been able to block the reintroduction of wolves. The wolf, however, should be reintroduced to Yellowstone National Park.

Focus: Write a Topic Sentence

One of the easiest ways to keep each paragraph focused on a single idea is to include a *topic sentence* in it, announcing or summarizing the topic of the paragraph, with the rest of the sentences supporting that main idea. Sometimes topic sentences conclude a paragraph, as in the previous example, where the topic sentence is also the thesis statement for the whole essay. More commonly, however, the topic sentence introduces the paragraph, as in the next example, also from Brendan's essay.

> Wolves need to be in Yellowstone in order to make it a complete ecosystem. Edward Lewis of the Greater Yellowstone Coalition, a regional conservation group, says that wolves are the missing link. They are the only major species which existed in historical times but is missing now. Wolves would help to balance the ecosystem by preying upon deer, elk, and moose. This would reduce the damage that overpopulation of these animals does to the area and limit the number of these species that starve during harsh winters.

The sentences after the first one support and amplify the topic sentence, explaining how wolves would make the park "a complete ecosystem."

Most of the following examples have topic sentences, and all focus on single subjects. Note, however, that not all paragraphs need topic sentences. For example, if a complicated idea is being explained, a new paragraph in the middle of the explanation will create a pause point. Sometimes paragraph breaks are inserted to emphasize an idea, like my own one-sentence paragraph, earlier, which is a topic and a support sentence all in one. Additionally, paragraphs in a personal experience essay seldom have a deliberate topic sentence since these sorts of essays are seldom broken into neat topics (see, for example, Judith's paragraph below). Nevertheless, in academic writing, there is great reverence for topic sentences because they point to clear organization and your ability to perform as an organized and logical thinker within the discipline. Thus, when you write academic papers, attend to topic sentences.

WRITING 1

Examine the paragraphs in a recent draft, and pencil in brackets around those that stick well to a single idea. Put an X next to any sentences that deviate from the main idea in a paragraph, and note whether you want to delete that sentence or use it to start a new paragraph. Finally, underline each topic sentence. If a paragraph does not have one, should it? If so, write it.

Order: Follow a Recognizable Logic

On first drafts, most of us write sentences rapidly and paragraph intuitively. However, when we revise and edit, it pays to make certain that paragraphs work according to a recognizable logic. There are dozens of organizational patterns that make sense; here we look at five of them: free association, rank order, spatial, chronological, and general to specific.

When ideas are organized according to *free association*, one idea triggers the next because it is a related one. Free association is especially common in advancing a narrative, as in a personal experience essay. It is quite fluid and suggestive and seldom includes topic sentences. In the following paragraph, Judith allows the first act of locking a door to trigger memories related to other locked doors.

> It is already afternoon. I fiddle with the key to lock the apartment door after me. I am not accustomed to locking doors. Except for the six months I spent in Boston, I have never lived in a place where I did not trust my neighbors. When I was little, we couldn't lock our farmhouse door; the wood had swollen, and the bolt no longer lined up properly with the hole, and nobody ever bothered to fix it. I still remember the time our babysitter, Rosie, hammered the bolt closed and we had to take the door off the hinges to get it open.

Notice that Judith uses a reverse chronological arrangement to order her associations, that is, she moves backward from the present — first to Boston, then to childhood — thereby using one pattern to strengthen another, helping us still further to follow her.

When ideas are arranged by *rank order*, that is, order of importance, the most significant idea is reserved for the end of the paragraph. The writer leads with the idea to be emphasized least, then the next most important, and so on. This paragraph is commonly introduced by a topic sentence alerting readers that an orderly list is to follow. Heather edited the following paragraph to summarize the importance of four ideas in her interpretive essay.

> These first two passages [in "Angelique's Letter"] are important in several ways. First, they show Angel's influence on his younger sister. Second, they introduce Angel's drive to make sure Angelique does not become pregnant and drop out of school "like the other girls in the neighborhood." Third, they show Angel's dedication to act on his resolve by turning innocent situations into lessons about inner-city life. Finally, the second passage ends with a clear warning that time is short, "And she was already talking about boys." If Angel wants to have an impact on his sister's life, he has to start now.

Notice that enumerating the ideas (first, second, etc.) helps readers keep track of each one. Heather could have edited her first sentence more sharply to set up the rest of the paragraph by replacing the vague phrase *in several ways* with the more precise *in four ways*, to reinforce the distinctiveness of each point. The result of paying attention to detail is improved readability.

When ideas are arranged *spatially*, each is linked to the next. Thus, the reader's eye is drawn through the paragraph as if through physical space. For example, a writer might describe a landscape by looking first at the field, then the forest, then the mountain, then the sky. In the following paragraph, Beth begins by showing Becky in the spatial context of her dormitory room; her description moves from bed to walls to floor.

> Becky sits cross-legged at the foot of the bottom bunk on her pink and green homemade quilt. She leans up against the wall and runs her fingers through her brown shoulder-length hair. The sound of James Taylor's "Carolina on my Mind" softly fills the room. Posters of John Lennon, James Dean, and Cher look down on us from her walls. Becky stares at the floor and scrunches her face as if she were thinking hard.

Becky's subtle, silent actions carry readers through the paragraph as Beth describes her sitting, leaning, listening, and staring — actions that set up the next paragraph in her paper in which Becky speaks.

When ideas or facts are arranged *chronologically*, they are presented in the order in which they happened, with the earliest first. Sometimes it makes sense to use *reverse chronology*, listing the most recent first and working backward in time. The following paragraph from a research paper illustrates normal chronology; it begins with the first microbrewery and then moves to a full-fledged brewers' festival five years later.

> According to Shaw (1990) the home brewing revolution did not begin in Vermont until February 1987 when Stephan Mason and Alan Davis opened Catamount Brewery, which offered golden lager, an amber ale, and a dark porter as well as several seasonal brews. This was only the beginning. In September 1992, the first Vermont Brewers Festival was held at Sugarbush Resort. Sixteen breweries participated and the forty-plus beers present ranged from American light lagers to German-style bock and everything in between. The beers included such colorful names as Tall Tale Pale Ale, Black Fly Stout, Slopbucket Brown Ale, Summer Wheat Ale, Avid Barley Wee Heavy, and Hickory Switch Smoked Amber Ale.

Notice that starting in the middle of the paragraph, another supportive pattern is at work here: the pattern of general to specific. It is unlikely that the first draft of this paragraph contained these mutually supportive organizational patterns; careful editing made sure the final draft did.

A *general to specific pattern* begins with an overall description or general statement and moves toward a description of smaller, more specific details. In the preceding paragraph, the general idea is "all breweries"; the specific idea is "Catamount beer."

The following two paragraphs in the same research essay are also organized general to specific, the first starting with the general category of brew pubs and moving to the specific Vermont Pub and Brewery, the next beginning with business in general and moving to Canadian business in particular.

> In addition to new breweries are brew pubs such as McNeill's Brewery in Brattleboro and the Vermont Pub and Brewery in Burlington. These are bars or restaurants which feature their own selection of beers brewed and served in-house only. Greg and Nancy Noonan, the owners of the Vermont Pub and Brewery, will be celebrating the fifth anniversary of their successful venture in December.
>
> According to Greg their business has been better than any of their predictions. He said, "Our first expectations were based on worst-case scenarios" (personal communication, November 17, 1992). In fact, for the Vermont Pub and Brewery there has not been any recession. Greg attributes this success to the consistency of the Burlington economic base and the increase of Canadian tourism: "Our Canadian business doubled or tripled since we opened on November 11, 1988."

Notice that the second paragraph does not start in a different direction or with a different topic from those in the first paragraph, though it is unified and has its own topic sentence. Instead it provides specific support for paragraph 1; its unifying subject is the speaker, Greg Noonan. In a previous draft, this paragraph was connected to the previous one; a new paragraph was created to hold the focus on the brewery. When we consider both paragraphs together, however, the principal organization of general to specific continues — from brew pubs in general to a specific brew pub to a specific brew pub owner talking.

Note, too, that *specific to general*, the reverse of the previous pattern, is also common and has a recognizable logic. For example, the brewery paper could have begun with two people sharing a specific beer in a specific pub; the writer then could have moved on to a description of the industry as a whole. The point here, as it is in all writing, is to edit carefully for pattern so that you lead your reader through the paper.

HELPING THE READER

Most of this discussion has focused so far on structures within paragraphs. When editing, it's important to know how to rewrite paragraphs to improve essay readability. However, you can improve readability in other ways as well. One of them is to break up lengthy paragraphs.

Paragraph breaks help readers pause and take a break while reading, allowing them, for example, to imagine or remember something sparked by the text and yet find their place again with ease. Breaking into a new paragraph can also recapture flagging attention, especially important in long essays, reports, or articles where detail sometimes overwhelms readers. And you can emphasize points with paragraph breaks, calling a little extra attention to what follows.

WRITING 2

Review a near-final draft of a paper you are working on, and identify the organizational pattern in each paragraph. Do you find a pattern to your paragraphing? Identify paragraphs that contain a single idea carefully developed and paragraphs that need to be broken into smaller paragraphs. What editing changes would you now make in the light of this review?

TRANSITIONS BETWEEN PARAGRAPHS

Your editing is not finished until you have linked the paragraphs, so that readers know where they have been and where they are going. In early drafts, you undoubtedly focused on getting your ideas down and paid less attention to clarifying relationships between ideas. Now, as you edit your final draft, consider the elements that herald transitions: words and phrases, subheads, and white spaces.

WORDS AND PHRASES. Writers often use transitional expressions without consciously thinking about them. For example, in writing a narrative, you may naturally use sequential transition words to indicate a chronology: *first, second, third; this happened, next this happened, finally this happened;* or *last week, this week, yesterday, today.* Here are some other transitional words and phrases and their functions in paragraphs:

Contrast or change in direction: *but, yet, however, nevertheless, still, at the same time, on the other hand*

Comparison or similarity: *likewise, similarly*

Addition: *and, also, then, next, in addition, furthermore, finally*

Summary: *finally, in conclusion, in short, in other words, thus*

Example: *for example, for instance, to illustrate, specifically, thus*

Concession or agreement: *of course, certainly, to be sure, granted*

Time sequence: *first, second, third; (1), (2), (3); next, then, finally, soon, meanwhile, later, currently, eventually, at last*

Spatial relation: *here, there, in the background, in the foreground, to the left, to the right, nearby, in the distance, above, below*

There is no need to memorize these functions or words; you already know and have used all of them and usually employ them quite naturally. When reworking your final draft, though, be sure you have provided transitions. If you haven't, work these words in to alert your readers to what's coming next.

ALTERNATE TRANSITIONAL DEVICES. Other common devices that signal transitions include subheadings, lines, alternate typefaces, and white spaces. The first two are more common in textbooks and technical reports, the latter two may appear in any text, including literary-style essays. When you edit your final draft, consider if using any of these techniques would make your ideas clearer.

SUBHEADS. To call extra attention to material or to indicate logical divisions of ideas, some writers use subheads. They are more common in long research papers, technical reports, and laboratory analyses and less common in narrative essays. They are essential in textbooks, such as this one, for indicating divisions of complex material.

LINES. Blocks of text can be separated by either continuous or broken dashes (-------) or asterisks (*****), which signify material clearly to be set off from other material. In technical writing, for example, material may even be boxed in by continuous lines to call special attention to itself. In a *New Yorker* research essay or short story, a broken line of asterisks may suggest a switch in time, place, or point of view.

ALTERNATE TYPEFACES.   Writers who use computers can change fonts with ease. When they use alternate typefaces, they are indicating a transition or a change. In a narrative or essay, *italics* may suggest someone talking or the narrator thinking aloud. A switch to a smaller or larger typeface may signal information of less or more importance.

WHITE SPACE.   You can indicate a sharp break in thought between one paragraph and the next by leaving an extra line of space between them (although the space break does not tell the reader what to expect next). When I use a space break, I am almost always suggesting a change in direction more substantial than a mere paragraph indentation; I want readers to notice the break and be prepared to make a larger jump than a paragraph break signals. In a narrative essay, I may use the space to suggest a jump in time (the next day, week, or year); in argumentative writing, to begin a presentation of an opposing point of view; in any essay, to introduce another voice. White space, in other words, substitutes for clear transition words and subheadings but does not explicitly explain the shift.

When I work on early drafts, I may use some of these transition or separation devices to help me keep straight the different parts of what I'm writing. In final drafts, I decide which devices will help my readers as much as they have helped me, and I eliminate those that no longer work. In other words, paragraphs and transitions are as useful for me when I'm drafting as they will be later for my readers.

WRITING 3

When you edit a final draft, look carefully at your use of transitional devices. Identify those that are doing their work well; add new ones where appropriate.

PARAGRAPHS AND THE ESSAY EXAM

Paragraph breaks, topic sentences, and transition and separation devices can have a marked impact on the readability of your answers on essay exams. Make an indentation each time you make a new point, so your reader will be sure to see each point. Use white space to emphasize a shift in topic or direction. (See Reference 3 for more information on essay examinations.)

Chapter 11
Opening and Closing

I could start this essay just about anywhere at all,
by telling you about the background, by stating the thesis, by telling
a funny story, or even by rambling, which is what I usually do.
Where do you think I should start?

– WENDY

M Y ADVICE, WENDY, is to lead with your best punch. Make your opening so strong your reader feels compelled to continue. Make your closing so memorable that your reader can't forget it.

Readers pay special attention to openings and closings, so make them work for you. Start with titles and lead paragraphs that grab readers' attention and alert them to what is to come; end with closings that sum up and reinforce where they've been. This chapter looks closely at how these special paragraphs function and how you can make these paragraphs stronger through skillful editing.

OPENINGS

Openings are first impressions. Your first paragraph — in fact, your whole first page — sets readers up for the rest of the paper. Here you provide the first clues about your subject, purpose, and voice and invite your audience to keep reading.

Good opening paragraphs are seldom written in first drafts. Often, it's not until you've finished a draft or two that you know exactly what your paper says and does. So when your paper is nearly finished, return to your first page, read it again, and edit carefully. The following examples of effective openings are taken from the student papers reproduced earlier in this textbook; all of them were rewritten at the editing stage.

Open with the Thesis Statement

Traditional college papers often open with a clear thesis statement that the rest of the paper will demonstrate. The following first paragraph from Heather's interpretive essay was edited extensively until it summarized the paper precisely and concluded with the thesis that the rest of the paper illustrates.

> "Angelique's Letter" tells a story about how a Puerto Rican college student named Angel decides to see his nine-year-old sister Angelique grow up having pride in herself and her culture, despite the disadvantages she will have to face throughout her life because of her race and economic background. Understanding the importance of education and achievement, Angel sets out to instill in his sister a sense of value towards these things, hoping that he will help her become all that she is capable of being.

Summary and thesis writing are among the most difficult of all writing tasks and for that reason are best written only when you are thoroughly familiar with your subject, which is seldom the case with early drafts. Hone your thesis statement to the sharpest possible sentence — this work will take a fair amount of effort — and then use it to conclude your opening paragraph.

Open with a Story

Most readers enjoy stories. Professional writers often open articles with anecdotes to catch readers' attention. The following first paragraph is from Judith's reflective essay about finding a safe place to study in the library. Only in her last draft did she decide to start at the door, in present tense, locking up. Then she edited carefully to bring readers with her as she developed her theme about the importance of personal safety.

> It is already afternoon. I fiddle with the key to lock the apartment door after me. I am not accustomed to locking doors. Except for the six months I spent in Boston, I have never lived in a place where I did not trust my neighbors. When I was little, we couldn't lock our farmhouse door; the wood had swollen, and the bolt no longer lined up properly with the hole, and nobody ever bothered to fix it. I still remember the time our babysitter, Rosie, hammered the bolt closed and we had to take the bolt off the hinges to get it open.

Open with a Specific Detail

Specific details appeal to readers' visual sense and help them see situations and settings. In early drafts, Beth opened her profile of Becky with Becky speaking; only in this latest version did she decide to set the physical scene first, letting Becky's manner and surroundings characterize her right from the start.

> Becky sits cross-legged at the foot of the bottom bunk on her pink and green homemade quilt. She leans up against the wall and runs her fingers through her brown shoulder-length hair. The sound of James Taylor's "Carolina on my Mind" softly fills the room. Posters of John Lennon, James Dean, and Cher look down on us from her walls. Becky stares at the floor and scrunches her face as if she were thinking hard.

Open with a Quotation

Although Beth decided not to open with her subject talking, an opening quotation can be an effective hook. Readers enjoy hearing the voices of people on the subject of the piece.

The following paragraph was Beth's original opening; she moved it to the second paragraph, adding the transitional first sentence to link the two paragraphs. (It would work equally well as her opening, since it introduces the reader to Becky's lively and interesting human voice, after which we expect more talk about her early years growing up "forever" with her mother and sister.)

> Finally, after minutes of silence [Becky] says, "I don't ever remember my father ever living in my house, really. He left when I was three and my sister was just a baby, about a year old. My mom took care of us all. Forever, it was just Mom, Kate, and me. I loved it, you know. Just the three of us together."

Sometimes it's just a matter of personal preference in deciding where to start. That, of course, is what editing is all about: trying one thing, then another, looking at options, in the end selecting the one that you think is best.

Open with an Interesting Statistic

Statistics that tell a clear story are another form of opening that suggests immediately that the writer has done his or her homework. The following sentences open the coauthored paper about the rise of the microbrewing industry in Vermont.

> The beer industry in the United States grosses forty billion dollars a year. Ninety-nine percent of those profits have been made by giant corporations such as Anheuser-Busch, Miller, and Coors (Mares, 1984, p. 112). But today, even though dollars are tight and industries are struggling to hold their ground, several microbreweries have gained a foothold in Vermont and they are fighting for their share of the profits (Shaw, 1990). This paper examines the options available to the Vermont beer drinker and explains what distinguishes these locally produced beers from their national competitors.

The more dramatic your statistics are, the more you should consider giving them prominence in your paper. In the preceding examples, the writers might have added one more sentence (always, more choices!) saying something like, "However, the new microbreweries, which today account for the 1 percent, are out to change that."

Open with a Question

Questions alert readers to the writer's subject and imply that the answer will be forthcoming in the paper. In the following example, Zoe leads with a simple question for readers to consider — and a question she intends to answer by becoming a professional photographer.

What makes a good advertising photograph?

Most writers ask unstated questions as the basis for their writing. For example, the microbrewery paper implicity asks, "Why are microbreweries popular?" Beth's profile asks, "What is Becky like?" and Judith asks, "What has scholarship to do with safety?"

WRITING 1

Recast the opening of a paper you are currently working on using one or more of the suggestions in this section: a thesis, story, specific detail, quotation, interesting statistic, or provocative question. For your final draft, use the opening that pleases you most.

CLOSINGS

Closings are final impressions. Your concluding sentences, paragraphs, or the entire last page are your final chance to make the point of your paper stick in readers' minds. The closing can summarize your main point, draw a logical conclusion, speculate about the issues you've raised, make a recommendation for some further action, or leave your reader with yet another question to ponder.

After writing and revising your paper, attend once more to the conclusion, and consider if the final impression is the one you want. You may discover an earlier paragraph makes a more suitable ending, or you may need to write a new one to conclude what you've started. The following examples of effective closings are from student papers reproduced earlier in this textbook.

Close with a Summary Statement

The end of your paper is a good place to summarize the point of your paper. The following paragraph concludes Keith's investigation into the high cost of compact discs.

> So the next time you walk into Record Land, you know what you
> are paying for. A CD may be twice as expensive as a record, but the
> sound is twice as clear and the disc will last forever.

This conclusion closes a frame for Keith's paper, since his first paragraph invited readers to consider why CDs cost so much. Writers often develop such frames, a setting or idea in which the main part of the story takes place, in the final stages of writing to attract audience attention, and conclude by returning the essay to the place from which it started.

Close with a Logical Conclusion

Many argumentative papers present first one side of an issue and then the other side, ending by drawing conclusions that reasonable readers could be expected to believe. The final paragraph of Brendan's position paper draws the conclusion that wolves should be reintroduced into Yellowstone National Park.

> The reintroduction of wolves into Yellowstone National Park is
> both an important and reasonable proposal. In this age of environmental abuse and excessive development by human beings, it seems only
> appropriate to set aside areas for the complete preservation of nature.
> Our National Parks are the ideal place for this. The wolf was once an
> integral part of the Yellowstone environment. Its reintroduction would
> complete the ecosystem and improve the natural situation. The arguments posed by farmers and hunters are insubstantial. An act of
> Congress requires government agencies to return the wolf to its original
> habitat. Why, then, are there still no wolves in Yellowstone?

In argumentative papers, with two reasonable sides to an issue, use your most careful and precise language when you draw conclusions. For this reason, it's especially important to edit carefully at the very end of your paper, assessing the impact of your final words on your audience.

Close with a Real or a Rhetorical Question

When you close a paper with a question, you invite readers to give the answer you've led them to. The final sentence of Brendan's wolf paper asks a rhetorical question, which he expects readers to answer in a predictable manner.

> Why, then, are there still no wolves in Yellowstone?

Another effective way to end is to pose unanswered questions that you have not investigated, in this way inviting readers to take the issue further. For example, Brendan might have asked similar questions about the disappearance of other large predators, such as mountain lions, from other national parks or about the disappearance of wolves from parks in the eastern United States.

Close with a Speculation

In papers relating personal experience, reflection, or speculation, the issues you raise have no clear-cut conclusions or demonstrated theses. In these papers, then, the most effective conclusion is often one in which you admit some uncertainty, as Zoe does at the end of her investigation of about becoming a photographer's assistant.

> So I'll keep sitting around hoping for a break. I can't guarantee that this research method for landing an internship will work; it still remains to be tried and tested. To my knowledge, there is no foolproof formula for a successful start. Like everybody else before me, I'm creating my own method as I go along.

The casualness in such a paragraph, as if it were written off the cuff, is often deceptive. While that is the effect Zoe wanted to create, this paragraph emerged only late in her drafting process, and when it did, she edited and reedited it to achieve just the effect she wanted.

Close with a Recommendation

Sometimes writers conclude by inviting their readers to do something — to support some cause, for example, or take some action. For example, the Yellowstone wolf paper could have ended by urging readers to petition their legislator to support a bill on behalf of the wolves. The end of the research essay on Ben and Jerry's ice cream makes a subtle recommendation for the kind of business the writers hope will characterize the next century.

> Ben and Jerry's is a growing enterprise which shows promising signs of worldwide expansion, not only for its excellent ice cream, but for its responsibility as well. Through caring capitalism Ben and Jerry have gained the support of both environmentalists and the business community. We believe Ben and Jerry's provides a good model of corporate responsibility as America enters the twenty-first century.

Close by Completing a Frame

An effective way to end some papers is to return to the issue or situation with which you began — to frame the body of your paper with an opening and a closing that mirror each other. Keith's CD paper used as a frame a customer considering the cost of a CD. Judith uses a frame in her paper about personal safety, returning in the closing to the setting of the opening — her front door.

> Hours later--my paper started, my exam studied for, my eyes tired--I retrace the path to my apartment. It is dark now, and I listen closely when I hear footsteps behind, stepping to the sidewalk's edge to let a man walk briskly past. At my door, I again fumble for the now familiar key, insert it in the lock, open the door, turn on the hall light, and step inside. Here, too, I am safe, ready to eat, read a bit, and finish my reflective essay.

FINDING THE TITLE

Finally, after revising and editing to your satisfaction, return to your title
and ask, Does it work? You want to make sure it sets up the essay to follow in
the best possible way, both catching readers' attention and providing a clue for
the content to follow.

One good strategy for deciding on a title is to create a list of five or ten
possibilities and then select the most suitable one. Play with words, arranging
and rearranging them until they strike you as just right. Many writers spend a
great deal of concentrated time on this task because titles are so important.
Following are seven tips:

1. Use one good sentence from your paper that captures the essence
   of your subject.
2. Ask a question that your paper answers.
3. Use a strong sense word or image from your paper.
4. Locate a famous line or saying that relates to your paper.
5. Write a one-word title (a two-word, a three-word title, and so on).
6. Make a title from a gerund (an -*ing* word, such as *brainstorming*).
7. Make a title starting with the word *on* and the name of your topic.

When I was casting about for a title for this book, I happened to be rid-
ing my motorcycle late one chilly October night on the interstate highway between Binghamton and Albany, New York. I was cold and knew I had a good
hour before arriving at my destination, so to distract myself from my discom-
fort I set about brainstorming titles and came up with "Writing to Discover" or
"The Discovering Writer." As I thought about them, I decided to keep the
word *writing* but to move away from *discover* toward *work*, and so played with
"The Writer Working," "Working Writers," "The Writer at Work," "Work and
the Writer." You know the result. Work hard to find the words that seem about
right, and play with them until they form a construction that pleases you.

Chapter 12
Working Sentences

Teachers are always nitpicking about little things, but I think
writing is for communicating, not nitpicking. I mean, if you
can read it and it makes sense, what else do you want?

– Omar

Omar, EDITING IS ABOUT NITPICKING. It's about making your text read well, with the most possible sense. After the ideas are in order and well supported, your job is to polish the paragraphs, sentences, and individual words so that they shine. Then you correct to get rid of all the "nitpicky" errors in punctuation, spelling, and grammar. In other words, you attend to editing *after* your ideas are conceptually sound, carefully supported, skillfully organized, and fairly well aimed at your readers. (Even now, it doesn't hurt to review it once more to make sure it represents your voice and ideas in the best way possible.)

In editing sentences, as in editing paragraphs, there is no one best way to go about this work. You edit in such a way that you remain, as much as possible, in control of your text. (As you probably know by now, texts have a way of getting away from all of us at times. Editing is how we try to get control back!) At the same time you're wrestling for final control of a text for yourself, you're also anticipating reader needs. In this sense, sentence editing is your final balancing act, as you work to please yourself and your readers.

EDITING FOR CLARITY, STYLE, AND GRACE

To effect maximum communication, you should edit your sentences first for clarity, making sure each sentence clearly reflects your purpose. You also must edit to convey an appropriate style for the occasion, that is, the formality or informality of the language. And at perhaps the highest level, you must edit to convey grace — some sense that this text is not only clearly written, by you, but that it is also particularly well written — what we might call elegant or graceful.

While I can explain this loose hierarchy as if these several levels are easily distinguished, in fact, they are not, and they mix and overlap easily. For instance, in writing the chapters for this text I have tried to edit each chapter, paragraph, and sentence with all three goals in mind, demanding that all my language is clear, hoping that my style is friendly and that my sentences are also graceful — knowing that, in many cases, grace has proved beyond my reach. The remainder of this chapter will examine the fine tuning of words and phrases that make clear, stylistically appropriate, and sometimes graceful sentences.

WRITING 1

Reread a near-final draft of one of your papers, and draw a straight vertical line next to places where your text seems especially clear. Draw a wavy line next to passages where the style sounds especially like you. And put an asterisk next to any passages that you think are especially graceful. Exchange drafts with a classmate and see if you agree with each other's assessment.

THE WORK OF SENTENCES

Sentences are written in relation to other sentences, so most of our attention thus far has been on larger units of composition, from whole texts on down to individual paragraphs. This chapter focuses on strategies for strengthening sentences. In editing, you should first look at the effect of particular words within sentences, especially nouns, verbs, and modifiers. Second, you should consider the importance of rhythm and emphasis in whole sentences. And finally, you should learn to identify and avoid the common problems of wordiness, clichés, jargon, passive constructions, and biased language.

Write with Concrete Nouns

Nouns label or identify persons (*man, Gregory*), animals (*dog, golden retriever*), places (*city, Boston*), things (*book, The Working Writer*), or ideas (*conservation, Greater Yellowstone Coalition*). General nouns name general classes or categories of things (*man, dog, city*); concrete nouns refer to particular things (*Gregory, golden retriever, Boston*). Notice that concrete nouns (not just any dog, but a golden retriever) appeal more strongly to a reader's senses (I can see the dog!) than abstract nouns do and create a more vivid and lively reading experience.

Here is an example of a paragraph composed primarily of general nouns (underlined in the passage).

> Approaching the library I see lots of <u>people</u> and <u>dogs</u> milling about, but
> no subjects to write about. I'm tired from my walk and go inside.

When Judith described a similar scene for her essay on personal safety, she used specific nouns (which are underlined) to let us see her story sharply.

> Approaching the library, I see <u>skateboarders</u> and <u>bikers</u> weaving
> through <u>students</u> who talk in clust<u>ers on the library steps</u>. A friendly
> black <u>dog</u> is tied to a <u>bench</u> watching for its master to return. Subjects
> to write about? Nothing strikes me as especially interesting and, be-
> sides, my heart is still pounding from the walk up the hill. I wipe my
> damp forehead and go inside.

Judith could have gone even further (writers always can) in using concrete nouns. She could have named the library, described some individual students, identified the dog, and described the bench. None of these modifications would have changed the essential meaning of the sentences, but each would have added a dimension of specific reality — one of the key ways writers convince readers that what they are writing about is true or really happened.

Write with Action Verbs

Action verbs *do* something in your sentences; they make something happen. *Walk, stride, run, jump, fly, hum, sing, sail, swim, lean, fall, stop, look, listen, sit, state, decide, choose,* and *conclude* — all these words and hundreds more are action verbs. Static verbs, in contrast, simply *appear* to describe how something *is* — like the verb *is* in this sentence. Action verbs, like concrete nouns, appeal to the senses, letting readers see, hear, touch, taste, or smell what is happening. They create more vivid images for readers, drawing them more deeply into the essay.

In the following passage, the conclusion to Judith's reflective essay, notice how action verbs (underlined) help you see clearly what is going on.

> Hours later--my paper started, my exam studied for, my eyes
> tired--I <u>retrace</u> the path to my apartment. It is dark now, and I <u>listen</u>
> closely when I <u>hear</u> footsteps behind, stepping to the sidewalk's edge to
> let a man <u>walk</u> briskly past. At my door, I again <u>fumble</u> for the now
> familiar key, <u>insert</u> it in the lock, <u>open</u> the door, <u>turn</u> on the hall light,
> and <u>step</u> inside. Here, too, I am safe, ready to eat, read a bit, and fin-
> ish my reflective essay.

Judith also uses several static verbs (*is, am*) in other places; these verbs describe necessary states of being, carrying a different kind of weight. When they are used among action verbs, they do good work. But the paragraph gets its life and strength from the verbs that show action.

Editing for action verbs is one of the chief ways to cut unneeded words, thus increasing readability and vitality. Whenever you find one of the following noun phrases (in the first column) consider substituting an action verb (in the second column):

reach a decision	decide
make a choice	choose
hold a meeting	meet
formulate a plan	plan
arrive at a conclusion	conclude
have a discussion	discuss
go for a run	run

Use Modifiers Carefully and Selectively

Well-chosen modifiers can make both nouns and verbs more concrete and appealing to readers' senses. Words that modify — describe, identify, or limit — nouns are called *adjectives* (*damp* forehead); words that amplify verbs are called *adverbs* (listen *closely*). Modifiers convey useful clarifying information and make sentences vivid and realistic.

In the previous example paragraph, Judith could have added several more modifiers to nouns such as *man* (*tall, thin, sinister*) and *door* (*red, heavy wooden*). And she could have used modifiers with verbs such as *retrace* (*wearily, slowly*) and *fumble* (*nervously, expectantly*). Judith's writing would not necessarily benefit by these additions, but they are further possibilities for her to examine as she edits her near-final sentences. Sometimes adding modifiers to sentences distracts from rather than enhances a paragraph's purpose. And that's what editing is all about: looking carefully, trying out new possibilities, settling for the effect that pleases you most.

Not all modifiers are created equal. Specific modifiers that add descriptive information about size, shape, color, texture, speed, and so on appeal to the senses and usually make writing more realistic and vivid. General modifiers such as the adjectives *pretty, beautiful, good, bad, ugly, young,* or *old* can weaken sentences by adding extra words that do not convey specific or vital information. And the adverbs *very, really,* and *truly* can have the same weakening effect because they provide no specific clarifying information.

WRITING 2

Review a near-final draft, and mark all concrete nouns (underline once), action verbs (underline twice), and modifiers (circle). Then place parentheses around the general nouns, static verbs, and general modifiers. Reconsider these words, and edit appropriately.

Find a Pleasing Rhythm

Rhythm is the pattern of sound sentences make when you read them out loud. Some rhythms sound natural — like a person in a conversation. Such sentences are easy to follow and understand and are usually pleasing to the ear. Others sound awkward and forced, make comprehension difficult, and offend the ear. It pays to read your sentences out loud and see if they sound like a real human being talking. To make sentence clusters sound better, use varied sentence patterns and parallel construction.

Varied sentence patterns make sentence clusters clear and enjoyable for readers. Judith effectively varied her sentences — some long, some short, some simple, some complex. For example, note the dramatic effect of following a lengthy compound sentence with a short simple sentence (made up of short words) to end the paragraph on page 353: "Nothing strikes me as especially interesting and, besides, my heart is still pounding from the walk up the hill. I wipe my damp forehead and go inside."

Parallelism, the repetition of a word or grammatical construction within a sentence, creates symmetry and balance, makes an idea easier to remember, and is pleasing to the ear. The following sentence from Brendan's essay demonstrates the pleasing rhythmic effect of parallel construction:

> A battle is being waged between environmental conservationists, who support the reintroduction of wolves, and sheep and cattle farmers and western hunters, who oppose it.

The parallelism is established by repetition of the word *who* plus a verb — and the verbs, opposite in meaning, provide additional dramatic effect.

In the following example, the repetition of the word *twice* establishes a rhythm and contributes as well to the writer's point about costs.

> A CD may be twice as expensive as a record, but the sound is twice as clear and the disc will last forever.

Place the Most Important Point Last

As in paragraphs so in sentences, the most emphatic place is last. You achieve the best effect by placing information that is contextual, introductory, or less essential earlier in the sentence and end with the idea you most want readers to remember. Sometimes you write first-draft sentences with emphatic endings, but often such emphasis needs to be edited in.

Notice the difference in emphasis in the following version of the same idea:

> Angel needs to start now if he wants to have an impact on his sister's life.

> If Angel wants to have an impact on his sister's life, he has to start now.

The second sentence is much more dramatic, emphasizing the need for action on Angel's part.

The next two sentences also illustrate the power of placing what you consider important at the end of the sentence:

> Becky stares at the floor and scrunches her face as if she were thinking hard.

> As if she is thinking hard, Becky stares at the floor and scrunches up her face.

The first sentence emphasizes Becky's concentration. To end with Becky's scrunching up her face diminishes the emphasis on her thinking.

In the following sentence, Judith uses end-of-sentence emphasis for a transitional purpose.

> I wipe my damp forehead and go inside.

The ending forecasts the next paragraph — in which Judith goes inside the library. To reverse the actions would emphasize the damp forehead instead of Judith's entrance into the library.

One more example from Judith's essay suggests how emphasis at the end can increase and then resolve suspense.

> It is dark now, and I listen closely when I hear footsteps behind, stepping to the sidewalk's edge to let a man walk briskly past.

At first we are alarmed that footsteps are coming up behind the writer — as Judith wants us to be. Then we are relieved that a man passes harmlessly by — as Judith also wants us to be. The end of the sentence relieves the tension and resolves the suspense.

WRITING 3

Examine the sentences in a recent draft for rhythm and end-of-sentence emphasis by reading the draft out loud, listening for awkward or weak spots. Edit for sentence variety and emphasis as necessary.

Edit Wordy Sentences

Cut out words that do not pull their weight or add meaning, rhythm, or emphasis. Sentences clogged with unnecessary words cause readers to lose interest, patience, and comprehension. Editing sentences for concrete nouns, action verbs, and well-chosen modifiers will help you weed out unnecessary words. Writing varied and emphatic sentences helps with this task too. Look at the following sentences, which all say essentially the same thing:

> In almost every situation that I can think of, with few exceptions, it will make good sense for you to look for as many places as possible to cut out needless, redundant, and repetitive words from the papers and reports, paragraphs and sentences you write for college assignments. [48 words]

> In most situations it makes good sense to cut out needless words from your college papers. [16 words]

> Whenever possible, omit needless words from your writing. [8 words]

> Omit needless words. [3 words]

The forty-eight-word-long first sentence is full of early-draft language; you can almost see the writer finding his or her way while writing. The sixteen-word sentence says much the same thing, with only one-third the number of words. Most of this editing simply cut out unnecessary words. Only at the end were several wordy phrases condensed: "from the papers and reports, paragraphs and sentences you write for college assignments" was reduced to "from your college papers."

That sixteen-word sentence was reduced by half by rephrasing and dropping the emphasis on college writing. And that sentence was whittled down by nearly two-thirds, to arrive at the core three-word sentence, "Omit needless words."

The first sentence was long-winded by any standard or in any context; each of the next three might serve well in different situations. Thus, when you edit to make language more concise, you need to think about the overall effect you intend to create. Sometimes the briefest construction is not the best one for your purpose. For example, the three-word sentence is more suited to a brief list than to a sentence of advice for this book. To fit the purposes of this book, in fact, I might write a fifth version on needless words, one including more of my own voice.

> I prefer to read carefully edited papers, where every word works purposefully and pretty much pulls its own weight. [19 words]

In this sentence, I chose to include *I* to emphasize my own preference as a teacher and reader and to add the qualifying phrase *pretty much* to impart a conversational tone to the sentence.

In the following example, one of Judith's effective paragraphs has been deliberately padded with extra words, some of which might have existed in earlier drafts.

> It is now several hours later, almost midnight, in fact. I have finally managed to get my paper started and probably overstudied for my exam. My eyes are very tired. I get up and leave my comfortable chair and walk out of the library, through the glass doors again, and retrace the path to my apartment. Since it is midnight, it is dark, and I nervously listen to footsteps coming up behind me. When they get too close for comfort, I step to the sidewalk's edge, scared out of my wits, to let a man walk briskly past. When I am finally at my door, I again fumble for the now familiar key, insert it in the lock, open the door, turn on the hall light, and step inside. Here, too, I am safe, ready to eat leftover pizza, study some more for my exam, and finish my reflective essay.

Now compare this with Judith's final version for simplicity, brevity, smoothness, and power.

> Hours later--my paper started, my exam studied for, my eyes tired--I retrace the path to my apartment. It is dark now, and I listen closely when I hear footsteps behind, stepping to the sidewalk's edge to let a man walk briskly past. At my door, I again fumble for the now familiar key, insert it in the lock, open the door, turn on the hall light, and step inside. Here, too, I am safe, ready to eat, read a bit, and finish my reflective essay.

The best test of whether words are pulling their own weight and providing rhythm, balance, and emphasis is to read the passage out loud and let your ear tell you what is sharp and clear and what could be sharper and clearer.

Edit Clichés

Clichés are phrases we've heard so often before that they no longer convey an original or individual thought. In the wordy paragraph above, the phrase "scared out of my wits" is a cliché. As you edit, note whether you remember hearing the same exact words before, especially more than once. If so, look for fresher language that is your own. Common clichés to avoid include the following:

throwing the baby out with the bath water

a needle in a haystack

the last straw

better late than never

without further ado

the handwriting on the wall

tried and true

last but not least

lay the cards on the table

jump start the economy

winning isn't everything

Each of these phrases was once new and original and attracted attention when it was used; now when we read or hear these phrases, we pay them no conscious mind and may even note that the writer or speaker using them is not very thoughtful or original.

Edit Passive Constructions

A construction is passive when something is done to the subject rather than the subject's doing something. *The ball was hit by John* is passive. *John hit the ball* is active. Not only is the first sentence needlessly longer by two words, it takes readers a second or two longer to understand since it is a roundabout way to make an assertion. Writing that is larded up with such passive constructions lacks vitality and is tiresome to read.

Most of the example paragraphs in this book contain good examples of active constructions: *I retrace . . . I get up . . . Becky sits . . . Greg attributes . . . He said . . .*

Edit Biased Language

Your writing should not hurt people. As you edit, make sure your language doesn't discriminate against categories of people based on gender, race, ethnicity, or social class.

ELIMINATE SEXISM.   Language is sexist when it includes only one gender. The most common occurrence of sexist language is the use of the word *man* or *men* to stand for *human being* or *people* — which seems to omit *women* from participation in the species. Americans have been sensitized to the not-so-subtle bias against woman embedded in our use of language.

It is important to remember that many thoughtful and powerful English-language works from the past took masculine words for granted, using *man, men, he, him,* and *his* to stand for all members of the human race. Consider Thomas Jefferson's "All men are created equal" and Tom Paine's "These are the times that try men's souls." Today we would write "All people are created equal" or "These are the times that try our souls" — two of several possible fixes for this gender nearsightedness. When you read older texts, recognize that the composing rules were different then and the writers no more at fault than the culture in which they lived.

As you edit to avoid sexist language, you will notice that the English language does not have a gender-neutral third-person singular pronoun to match the gender-neutral third-person plural (*they, their, them*). We use *he* (*him, his*) for men and *she* (*her, hers*) for women. In the sentence, "Everybody has his own opinion," the indefinite pronoun *everybody* needs a singular pronoun to refer to it. While it is grammatically correct to say "Everybody has his own opinion," the sentence seems to exclude women. But it is grammatically incorrect to write "Everybody has *their* own opinion," although *their* is gender neutral. In editing, be alert to such constructions and consider several ways to fix them:

- Make the sentence a plural so it reads: "*People* have *their* own opinions."
- Include both pronouns: "Everybody has *his or her* own opinion."
- Eliminate the pronoun: "Everybody has *an* opinion."
- Alternate masculine and feminine pronouns throughout your sentences or paragraphs, using *she* in one paragraph and *he* in the next.

In my own writing, I have used all of these solutions at one time or another. The rule I most commonly follow is to use the strategy that makes for the clearest, most graceful writing.

AVOID STEREOTYPES.   Stereotypes lump individuals into oversimplified and usually negative categories based on race, ethnicity, class, gender, sexual preference, religion, or age. You know many of these terms. The kindest are perhaps "Get out of the way old man" and "Don't behave like a baby." I am willing to set these down in this book since we've all been babies and we're all growing older. The other terms offend me too much to write.

The mission of all institutions of higher learning is to teach you to read, write, speak, and think critically, which means treating each situation, case, problem, or person individually on its own merits and not prejudging it by rumor, innuendo, or hearsay unsupported by evidence or reason. To use stereotypes in academic writing will label you as someone who has yet to learn critical literacy. To write with stereotypes in any setting not only reveals your ignorance but hurts people.

Proofread

The last act of editing is proofreading, the process of reading your manuscript word for word to make sure it is correct in every way. Here are some tips to help you in this process:

- Proofread for typing and spelling errors first by using a spelling checker on your computer, if you have one. But be aware that computers will *not* catch certain errors, such as omitted words or mistyping (e.g., *if* for *of*). So you must also proofread the old-fashioned way — by reading slowly, line by line, word by word.
- Proofread for punctuation by reading your essay out loud and looking for places where your voice pauses, comes to a full stop, questions, or exclaims. Let your verbal inflections suggest appropriate punctuation (commas, periods, question marks, and exclamation points, respectively). Also review the punctuation reference at the end of this book, paying special attention to the use of commas, the most common source of punctuation errors.
- Proofread the work of others, and ask others to proofread for you. It's easy when reading your own writing to fill in missing words and read through small errors; you're much more likely to catch such errors in someone else's writing. We are all our own worst proofreaders; ask somebody you trust to help you.
- Proofread as a whole class: Tape final drafts on the wall, and roam the class with pencils reading one another's final drafts, for both pleasure and correctness.

WRITING 4

Examine a recent draft for wordiness, clichés, passive constructions, and biased language. Edit as necessary according to the suggestions in this section. Proofread before you hand in or publish the paper.

Chapter 13
Additional Materials
Student Information Survey

Your Name:

Your year and major (declared or anticipated):

What are your goals for this course:

Which of the works from the syllabus, if any, have you previously read or studied?

What kinds of things do you read for pleasure or interest?

What book or books has been most significant to your intellectual development?

What are some of your other interests?

Is there anything else you think I should know about you as a student?

Do you use a computer for writing? If so, your own or in a lab?

Do you have an e-mail address?

Student Information Survey

Your Name:

Your year and major (declared or anticipated):

What are your goals for this course:

Which of the works from the syllabus, if any, have you previously read or studied?

What kinds of things do you read for pleasure or interest?

What book or books has been most significant to your intellectual development?

What are some of your other interests?

Is there anything else you think I should know about you as a student?

Do you use a computer for writing? If so, your own or in a lab?

Do you have an e-mail address?

Peer Review Checklist

Writer:

Reviewer:

Read the essay once to get a general idea of the writer's point. While you are reading, indicate in the margin (with a check mark or something similar) any places where you find examples of:

—unclear or illogical wording

—superficial grammatical errors

—awkward sentences

Then read the essay a second time, more slowly, and answer the following questions as thoroughly as possible in the time available. Your teacher may modify or add to these questions to accommodate a particular paper assignment.

1. Does the essay fulfill the assignment? If the draft doesn't yet, why not?

2. Is the thesis of the essay clear? Is it clear why the writer holds it? Make suggestions for improvement.

3. Is the argument in support of the thesis offered in a persuasive way without sounding too obvious or too farfetched? Is there sufficient evidence from the text? Can the writer's evidence be interpreted in some other way? Make suggestions for improvement.

4. What questions about or possible objections to the argument do you have? If you are persuaded, try to answer this question from the perspective of someone who remains skeptical.

5. How could the beginning and end of the essay be improved?

6. What do you see as the major strengths of this interpretation?

Peer Review Checklist

Writer:

Reviewer:

Read the essay once to get a general idea of the writer's point. While you are reading, indicate in the margin (with a check mark or something similar) any places where you find examples of:

—unclear or illogical wording

—superficial grammatical errors

—awkward sentences

Then read the essay a second time, more slowly, and answer the following questions as thoroughly as possible in the time available. Your teacher may modify or add to these questions to accommodate a particular paper assignment.

1. Does the essay fulfill the assignment? If the draft doesn't yet, why not?

2. Is the thesis of the essay clear? Is it clear why the writer holds it? Make suggestions for improvement.

3. Is the argument in support of the thesis offered in a persuasive way without sounding too obvious or too farfetched? Is there sufficient evidence from the text? Can the writer's evidence be interpreted in some other way? Make suggestions for improvement.

4. What questions about or possible objections to the argument do you have? If you are persuaded, try to answer this question from the perspective of someone who remains skeptical.

5. How could the beginning and end of the essay be improved?

6. What do you see as the major strengths of this interpretation?

Peer Review Checklist

Writer:

Reviewer:

Read the essay once to get a general idea of the writer's point. While you are reading, indicate in the margin (with a check mark or something similar) any places where you find examples of:

—unclear or illogical wording

—superficial grammatical errors

—awkward sentences

Then read the essay a second time, more slowly, and answer the following questions as thoroughly as possible in the time available. Your teacher may modify or add to these questions to accommodate a particular paper assignment.

1. Does the essay fulfill the assignment? If the draft doesn't yet, why not?

2. Is the thesis of the essay clear? Is it clear why the writer holds it? Make suggestions for improvement.

3. Is the argument in support of the thesis offered in a persuasive way without sounding too obvious or too farfetched? Is there sufficient evidence from the text? Can the writer's evidence be interpreted in some other way? Make suggestions for improvement.

4. What questions about or possible objections to the argument do you have? If you are persuaded, try to answer this question from the perspective of someone who remains skeptical.

5. How could the beginning and end of the essay be improved?

6. What do you see as the major strengths of this interpretation?

Peer Review Checklist

Writer:

Reviewer:

Read the essay once to get a general idea of the writer's point. While you are reading, indicate in the margin (with a check mark or something similar) any places where you find examples of:

—unclear or illogical wording

—superficial grammatical errors

—awkward sentences

Then read the essay a second time, more slowly, and answer the following questions as thoroughly as possible in the time available. Your teacher may modify or add to these questions to accommodate a particular paper assignment.

1. Does the essay fulfill the assignment? If the draft doesn't yet, why not?

2. Is the thesis of the essay clear? Is it clear why the writer holds it? Make suggestions for improvement.

3. Is the argument in support of the thesis offered in a persuasive way without sounding too obvious or too farfetched? Is there sufficient evidence from the text? Can the writer's evidence be interpreted in some other way? Make suggestions for improvement.

4. What questions about or possible objections to the argument do you have? If you are persuaded, try to answer this question from the perspective of someone who remains skeptical.

5. How could the beginning and end of the essay be improved?

6. What do you see as the major strengths of this interpretation?

In-Progress Feedback Sheet

At the end of the quarter you will have a chance to evaluate the course. Because feedback during the quarter can be useful to both you and your teacher, you may be asked to complete this survey at some point during Great Books. Your teacher will read your responses carefully and take them into account as he or she plans the rest of the quarter. You don't need to sign the sheet unless you want to.

1. Which of the course objectives do you feel you are making good progress toward so far? With which of them would you like additional guidance or help?

2. Which of the objectives is personally most important to you? Which is least important?

3. Which activities or requirements have been most helpful to you? Least helpful? Consider here such activities as daily written work (quizzes, brief writings), class discussion, group work, lectures, essay assignments, classes devoted to the writing process, conferences with your teacher.

4. Are there other comments and ideas you would like your teacher to consider? Please feel free to write on the back of this page.

In-Progress Feedback Sheet

At the end of the quarter you will have a chance to evaluate the course. Because feedback during the quarter can be useful to both you and your teacher, you may be asked to complete this survey at some point during Great Books. Your teacher will read your responses carefully and take them into account as he or she plans the rest of the quarter. You don't need to sign the sheet unless you want to.

1. Which of the course objectives do you feel you are making good progress toward so far? With which of them would you like additional guidance or help?

2. Which of the objectives is personally most important to you? Which is least important?

3. Which activities or requirements have been most helpful to you? Least helpful? Consider here such activities as daily written work (quizzes, brief writings), class discussion, group work, lectures, essay assignments, classes devoted to the writing process, conferences with your teacher.

4. Are there other comments and ideas you would like your teacher to consider? Please feel free to write on the back of this page.

In-Progress Feedback Sheet

At the end of the quarter you will have a chance to evaluate the course. Because feedback during the quarter can be useful to both you and your teacher, you may be asked to complete this survey at some point during Great Books. Your teacher will read your responses carefully and take them into account as he or she plans the rest of the quarter. You don't need to sign the sheet unless you want to.

1. Which of the course objectives do you feel you are making good progress toward so far? With which of them would you like additional guidance or help?

2. Which of the objectives is personally most important to you? Which is least important?

3. Which activities or requirements have been most helpful to you? Least helpful? Consider here such activities as daily written work (quizzes, brief writings), class discussion, group work, lectures, essay assignments, classes devoted to the writing process, conferences with your teacher.

4. Are there other comments and ideas you would like your teacher to consider? Please feel free to write on the back of this page.

In-Progress Feedback Sheet

At the end of the quarter you will have a chance to evaluate the course. Because feedback during the quarter can be useful to both you and your teacher, you may be asked to complete this survey at some point during Great Books. Your teacher will read your responses carefully and take them into account as he or she plans the rest of the quarter. You don't need to sign the sheet unless you want to.

1. Which of the course objectives do you feel you are making good progress toward so far? With which of them would you like additional guidance or help?

2. Which of the objectives is personally most important to you? Which is least important?

3. Which activities or requirements have been most helpful to you? Least helpful? Consider here such activities as daily written work (quizzes, brief writings), class discussion, group work, lectures, essay assignments, classes devoted to the writing process, conferences with your teacher.

4. Are there other comments and ideas you would like your teacher to consider? Please feel free to write on the back of this page.